The Evangelizing Parish

Theologies and Strategies for Renewal

Patrick J. Brennan

A Resource for Parish Staffs and Leaders

TABOR
PUBLISHING
Allen, TX   Valencia, CA

Book design by Bonnie Baumann
Cover design by Design Office

Send all inquiries to:
Tabor Publishing
25115 Avenue Stanford, Suite 130
Valencia, California 91355

Printed in the United States of America

ISBN 0-89505-448-5

1 2 3 4 5   90 89 88 87 86

To Dawn,
valued friend, trusted associate

CONTENTS

Preface   vii

Acknowledgments   ix

Introduction Fundamentalists, Evangelicals, and Catholics   1

   1 What Is Catholic Evangelization?   5

   2 Evangelizing Active Parishioners   23

   3 Inactive or Alienated Parishioners:
      New Dimensions for Ministry of Care   63

   4 Evangelizing Youth   97

   5 The Catechumenal Parish   109

Index   115

PREFACE

The title and subtitle of this book indicate how I personally approach evangelization. Though there has been an explosion of ministries in the past twenty years, the parish continues to be, in America, the tool with the greatest potential for touching people's lives. The subtitle indicates that this book deals with both theology and strategies, or models, for evangelizing. I include both, because theology provides a *why* for the *what* of models or strategies. The subtitle also gives a description of the people that I feel are in most need of a resource book like this: pastors, staffs, and parishioner leaders—anyone who cares about the future of the Church and the coming of God's Kingdom.

Cardinal Suenens, in a presentation at the Extraordinary Synod of Bishops in the fall of 1985, earnestly called for a serious, conscious emphasis on evangelization in the Roman Catholic Church. His intensity came from a conviction that he and others have had. The world and the Church of today stand in greater need of evangelizing efforts than the world and the Church of Vatican II days. Since the 1960s there have been major shifts in the quality and style of family life, the support that culture and society provide for Christian values, and the influence that the Church has on the daily lives of people. There are some people who say that we are in a post-Christian era, one in which the followers of Jesus live in an increasingly idolatrous world. If this book makes a small contribution toward a renewal of evangelization, I will be most pleased.

Patrick J. Brennan

ACKNOWLEDGMENTS

The Evangelizing Parish has its origins in many different people, parishes, and experiences. My interest in evangelization began in the mid-seventies when I served as both associate pastor and director of religious education at St. Hubert parish in Hoffman Estates, Illinois. While holding two such positions was neither healthy nor reflective of good staff practice, it placed me in a position to develop a number of creative and innovative approaches to religious education and youth ministry. This innovation, especially in the area of evangelization, grew out of a growing dissatisfaction that I had as DRE and priest with the status quo of most typical parish programs. It more and more seemed to me that we were pushing families, teens, and young people through programmatic hoops, with little evidence that their lives were changed. Sacraments and preparation for them had become some sort of cultural milestones, but certainly not celebrations of individual or familial conversion.

It was during the course of this period of discontent that Paul VI issued his document on evangelization, *Evangelii Nuntiandi.* This document provided the "missing link" in so many of my parish efforts—conscious, up-front evangelizing. Neither in attitude nor in practice had I been evangelizing, calling people to root their lives in Jesus. This new awareness helped me devise a number of new strategies and approaches for ministry and religious education. I should note here that while this awareness did result in beginning some new processes, programs, and ministries, it also included much fine-tuning of what the parish was already doing in school, CCD, sacramental preparation, and youth ministry. In other words, it was not necessary to bulldoze already existing efforts at St. Hubert's. Rather, the transition to become a more evangelizing parish involved placing evangelization as a lens or filter through which we would continue, change, and improve already existing ministries. Sections of *The Evangelizing Parish* explain how this happened over the course of some years. *Years* is an important word here. To effectively change parish systems requires several years of patient attention, study, and prayer, and a great deal of collaboration and cooperation. I am grateful to the staffs and people of St. Hubert's for providing such a rich laboratory for beginning my evangelizing efforts.

I am also indebted to the staff and people of St. Albert the Great in Burbank, Illinois. Though my time with them was short (two years), they patiently cooperated with me in adapting what I had learned at St. Hubert's to a radically different culture and style of parish. St. Albert's helped me discover those strategies and theories that seem to have universal application, despite the parish context, and those that were time and culture bound in my first assignment. The generosity and enthusiasm of many people in St. Albert's still amaze me. This parish continues to have one of the strongest programs of outreach to inactive and alienated members in the entire metropolitan area.

This "evangelization odyssey" would be incomplete without mentioning the people of St. Michael's, Orland Park, Illinois, where parishioners practice such great "ownership" over the ministries of the parish, under the able leadership of Msgr. John Gorman. St. John the Evangelist, in Streamwood, Illinois, is my recent laboratory, where Fr. Bill Moriarity, Sr. Kathleen LaPlume, and other staff and parish leaders are taking bold steps toward becoming an evangelizing parish.

It also has been a privilege to work with Fr. Michael Pfleger of St. Sabina in Chicago, who has helped me translate the ideas and skills contained in this book for the evangelization of black people, while valuing the beauty of the black culture. The same can be said for Fr. Ted O'Keefe and Fr. Pedro Rodriguez, who have become invaluable resources in developing materials for Hispanic evangelization. I wish to thank Joseph Cardinal Bernardin for his ongoing support of the Office for Chicago Catholic Evangelization; Mr. Richard C. Leach, chairman and publisher of DLM, Inc., and Mr. Cullen Schippe, president of Tabor Publishing, for their approval of this work.

On a more personal level, I am forever indebted to my parents, who first gifted me with faith, and to Fr. Jerry Broccolo (friend and spiritual advisor), who opened for me, as an adult, the richness of the Kingdom of God. And last but not least, my profound gratitude to Dawn Mayer, who stood by me and worked with me in the beginning of the Office for Chicago Catholic Evangelization, the National Council for Catholic Evangelization, and our most current endeavor, the National Center for Evangelization and Parish Renewal. She is an example of a true building block of the Church of the future.

INTRODUCTION
Fundamentalists, Evangelicals, and Catholics

The name *fundamentalist* was first used in a Baptist weekly newspaper called the *Watchman-Examiner*. It was used to describe a growing body of Christians who, as early as the end of the nineteenth century, were increasingly uncomfortable with liberal Protestant theology. From 1915 to 1920, R. A. Torrey progressively wrote a twelve-volume series entitled *The Fundamentals*. This earliest of fundamentalist literature did not have the tone of hostility that is present in much of the current fundamentalist materials. Rather, Torrey was trying to set forth and explain *the fundamentals* of Christian orthodoxy. Chief among these fundamental doctrines were (1) the infallibility and inspiration of the Bible, (2) the divinity of Christ, (3) the salvific effects of Christ's death on the cross, (4) the literal resurrection of Jesus from the dead, and (5) the literal return of Christ in the second coming.

Evangelicalism is a parallel movement. Since the eighteenth century, it has attracted people who ascribe to the doctrine of salvation by faith in Jesus alone. Evangelicals deny the value of either good works or sacraments. The essence of Christianity is faith in the atoning death and resurrection of Jesus. Evangelicalism became even more conservative in the early twentieth century. Many evangelicals aligned themselves with fundamentalists as they severed ties with mainline Protestant churches: Lutherans, Episcopalians, and Methodists. Evangelicals critique strict fundamentalists for their perceived lack of concern for social justice, and an elitism that is decidedly nonecumenical. There are some

1

Christians who are now considered "new evangelicals." They reject the negative, angry spirit of fundamentalism. In terms of doctrinal beliefs, fundamentalists and evangelicals are quite similar. However, they do differ in style and tone. Fundamentalists are frequently judgmental and critical toward Catholics and other Christians. Evangelicals are more open in their approach to other Christian bodies. Southern Baptists and other Baptists, Missouri Synod Lutherans, Christian Reformed, some Presbyterian churches, and many other groups are classified as "evangelical." *Christianity Today,* an ecumenical journal, maintains that there are 31 million American adults who are evangelicals. Four million of these also consider themselves Roman Catholic. Father Leonard Foley, O.F.M., who has done research in this area, estimates that 30 percent of American adults are fundamentalists. Reverend Jerry Falwell gives insight into fundamentalism in his assertion that fundamentalists alone are legitimate heirs of orthodox Christianity and biblical spirituality.

Fundamentalists and evangelicals are characterized by zeal, spirit, enthusiasm, and a missionary attitude toward their faith. Many fundamentalist and evangelical churches have well-organized evangelism programs in which parishioners are trained to lead people both to Christ and to their particular church community. Many of us have encountered these lay evangelists at meetings, at work, and in a variety of other situations in which some variation of the question "Are you saved?" has been put to us.

Evangelization, or evangelism as it is sometimes called, is the focal point of these churches. Some parishioners in these communities come forward to be trained in skills for evangelization. Others enter into a ministry of prayer for the work of the evangelizers. All, however, are united in the one mission of evangelizing.

The steps in evangelical training are rather similar in many of these communities. The training of the evangelizers, or callers, is extensive in length but simple in the skills that are shared. The main skills that are usually shared in training are described below.

Two Diagnostic Questions

Evangelizers need to discern whether a person is in need of conversion, whether he or she has been born again. Two diagnostic questions are practiced by the callers. The answers given to the questions tip the evangelizer as to whether the person is in need of a primary conversion.

- *Diagnostic question one.* If you died tonight, would you go to heaven?

If a person is born again, or "saved," he or she should promptly respond, "Yes, I would go to heaven." Many mainline Christians (like Catholics) or those who are not active in their faith respond either with "I don't know for sure" or "I hope so" or some other response that is lacking in conviction.

- *Diagnostic question two.* If you died tonight and went to heaven, why should God allow you into heaven?

If someone has said yes to the first question, this second question is designed to test the depth of his or her faith. The only acceptable response in evangelical thinking is that heaven is a free gift that comes through faith in Jesus Christ. Again, many Catholics and others in mainline churches claim that heaven is theirs because of something that *they did*: they kept the commandments; they went to church; and so on.

If people fail to answer one or both of the questions accurately, they are diagnosed as not saved, not born again; and evangelizers go on to use the rest of their skills.

Presentation of the Gospel

The core of the Good News is effectively packaged in a unique style by each evangelizer. This gospel presentation is put together in three pieces.

1. The evangelizer learns the core gospel message:
- People cannot save themselves.
- God must punish sin.
- Christ paid the price for sin with His atoning death.
- Eternal life is offered to us as a gift through Jesus.
- One must verbally accept Jesus as personal Lord and Savior, and invite Him into his or her heart to receive the gift of eternal life.

2. The above theology is wrapped into a personal witness story. The evangelizer shares how the above truth came alive in his or her life.

3. The evangelizer also shares memorized passages from Scripture that confirm and support the gospel message as it was filtered through the faith story described in 2, above.

Two Clarifying Questions

The evangelizer then asks two more questions.
- *Question one.* Does the personalized proclamation of the gospel that you just heard make sense?
- *Question two.* Do you want the same gift in your life?

Clarification of the Commitment

The evangelizer clarifies the nature of the commitment that the other person is about to make. The meaning of faith, the Lordship of Christ, and responsible membership in the church are clarified. Then the evangelizer leads the person in a prayer of commitment, which is usually similar to this:

> *"Lord Jesus, I am a sinful person. I am sorry for my sins. I want to turn away from them. I want you to be Lord and Savior of my life. Please, come and enter my heart."*

The prayer is said phrase by phrase by the evangelizer and repeated by the person who is in the process of being born again.

Assurance of Salvation

The evangelizer closes the time together by returning to the two diagnostic questions, pointing out to the newly born-again Christian that he or she indeed has the gift of eternal life and would immediately go to heaven.

The encounter between the evangelizer and the person on whom he or she calls is immediately followed up by multiple nurturing activities. The newly born-again Christian is visited by the pastor, invited to Bible study, invited to parish activities, and picked up by church members for weekend worship.

The strategies just described have been critiqued by many Catholic and Protestant observers. Among the issues raised by critics are (1) the automatic nature of conversion in this model, (2) the manipulative, judgmental attitudes inherent in this approach, and (3) the appeal to the fears and anxieties present in people in a nuclear age.

But we need to take note of some of the strengths of this model. Among them are (1) the emphasis on the marketplace, or the world, as the proper focus for evangelizing (these churches do not wait for people to come to them, but rather move out into the world); (2) the use of lay people who are empowered, enabled, and trained for evangelizing (the parish staff does not pretend to be able to accomplish the mission of evangelization themselves); (3) the simple and easily replicable skills used by the evangelizers; and (4) the fact that in these churches there are no observers (all are called to participate in the mission of evangelization). We have some things to learn from these evangelizers!

This short introduction on fundamentalist and evangelical evangelizing is intended to clarify a very popular style of evangelizing in our culture today, and also to initiate discussion on the evangelizing parish from a Catholic perspective.

What Is Catholic Evangelization?

For the past ten years, the word *evangelization* has popped up recurrently in Catholic literature and pastoral programs. I recently saw an extensive article on it in an eighth-grade religion book, in which junior high students were encouraged to become evangelizers. Catholics are apparently getting more comfortable with the word; they are beginning to, in effect, *own* the word. But evangelization remains an amorphous term. We use it; we talk about it; but we do not often stop to ask or discuss the meaning of this word. At a recent conference, a woman finally put up her hand, after about an hour and a half of listening to me, and asked, "What do you mean by evangelization? I'm still not sure." I hope this book is helpful in explaining what evangelization is and could be.

If evangelization is becoming more popularized, it is, however, with the more aware, well-read, or actively involved Catholic or family. For many Catholics, the term is rather foreign sounding. In fact, it may actually be an alienating word for some people who connect evangelization only with tent meetings, Bible thumping, or a "hard sell" approach to preaching or sharing the gospel. In my experience, the latter is perhaps the most common understanding of the word. And so, those of us actively involved in leadership in evangelization the past few years have, at least initially, had a few doors closed in our faces, because people presumed anyone involved in evangelization must be either an evangelical, a fundamentalist, or involved in charismatic renewal. In other words, evangelization is seen as the work or concern of an elite few, but not something that would be of interest to the vast majority of Catholics or Christians. One of the principles running through this study of evangelization is that evangelization *does have*, and indeed *must have*, universal implications for the entire Church, for each baptized Christian. Evangelization is the central mission of the Church in general, and of individual Christians in particular.

A TURNING POINT IN CATHOLIC EVANGELIZATION

The mid-seventies were turning-point years in evangelization. In 1974, the bishops met in synod in Rome on the topic of evangelization. A study document, entitled *The Evangelization of the Modern World*, was released around the time of the synod. The pastoral spoke of the spiritual hunger and thirst so evident in the world today, a hunger and thirst that can be satisfied only by the person of Jesus and His Good News. The bishops spoke of this era as a time ripe for renewed efforts at evangelization.

The bishops also realistically assessed the obstacles to a renewal of evangelization. Obstacles exist both inside and outside of the Church. Among the numerous "outside obstacles" listed were social changes that have affected communal and neighborhood structures, international tensions, the decline of traditional values, and a growing scientific attitude that excludes the values of the unmeasurable, growing atheism and secularization. Within the Church there are obstacles like frail, superficial faith; distortions of Christianity, Scripture, and theology; difficulty in translating Christian beliefs and values into the contemporary idiom; ecclesiastical structures that tend to hinder rather than reveal the gospel; Church leaders that become overly concerned with material goods and wealth; an increasingly pluralistic world and Church, which threaten to weaken a sense of Catholic unity.

In their document, the bishops list several commonly accepted connotations of the term *evangelization*. (1) Evangelization, in some Catholic circles, refers to every activity in which the world is transformed according to the gospel and the will of God. (2) For others, evangelization refers to any ministerial activity by which the Church is built up. (3) A third understanding is that evangelization is any activity by which the gospel is proclaimed and explained; and therefore, living faith is awakened in non-Christians and is nourished in those already Christian. (4) Still others rather narrowly define evangelization as the first step in the process of religious education, that is, the first proclamation of the gospel. Though the bishops built their vision on the third approach above, all four are quite acceptable within the Catholic tradition. A composite vision of all of them looks like this: *Evangelization is the proclamation of the gospel, to Christians and non-Christians, in an attempt to awaken and/or nourish faith. It also includes any activity directed toward the building up of the Church and the transformation of the world toward the gospel and the will of God.*

The bishops say that renewed interest in evangelization leads the Church directly into consideration of other related theological issues, namely, salvation, faith, conversion, the role of Jesus as the Christ, the Church, and ministry. Evangelization is essentially, in the bishops' view, our participation in the gradual revelation of the mystery of salvation. At the very center of this revelation is Jesus Christ. This ministry of revealing Christ and offering salvation is a mission that we have for the entire world. We fulfill the mission through proclamation, our sacramental life, and lives of witness. The response to evangelization that we seek from those evangelized is conversion and faith.

The bishops go on to share other concerns about evangelization in the modern world. These concerns are most often expressed in questions for the reader. Here I take the liberty to state my interpretation of these apparent concerns.

- As evangelizers we need to be concerned about qualitative and quantitative conversion. While our first concern must always be on the depth of conversion that a person experiences, we need to keep in mind the responsibility we have to share the gospel with all.
- We need to respect the wisdom in non-Christian traditions, and see such expressions as possible steps toward the full wisdom of the gospel.
- It is really the Holy Spirit, working through us, that is the agent of evangelization and conversion.
- Evangelization is not manipulative proselytism.
- Evangelization always builds on the culture of a local people. Evangelization ministries must not rob people of the truth and goodness of their culture. At the same time, evangelization does stand up against and critiques the illusions and sin of some cultures.
- Evangelization leads to a kind of death, and the beginning of a fuller life. The goal of evangelization is conversion.
- More than just an educational enterprise, evangelization must be oriented toward total human development and the transformation of the social order.

- Individual salvation and conversion, building up the Church, and transforming the world are three values to be kept in tension by evangelizers.
- Evangelization efforts must also be ecumenically sensitive.

The bishops' document closes with guidelines on how to engage in this mission and ministry of evangelization. Parishes, dioceses, priests' councils, religious orders and institutions, families, and universities are challenged to scrutinize their efforts in order to determine whether they are truly evangelizing forces. The Church as a whole is challenged to discern whether the media are being used sufficiently to further the mission of evangelization. Finally, attention is turned to the necessary connection between evangelization and social justice.

THE MAGNA CARTA OF EVANGELIZATION

The bishops' study document was a prelude to an even more influential work, Pope Paul's *Evangelii Nuntiandi* of 1975. This encyclical has significantly advanced the cause of evangelization in the Catholic Church. Paul VI saw a renewed effort at evangelization as a natural flowering of the work of the Second Vatican Council. He opens his encyclical with three fundamental questions: (1) What has happened to the hidden energy of the gospel which we know to be a powerful influence on human consciousness? (2) Is the gospel still capable of transforming lives? (3) What methods are needed in the future to insure that the gospel has its proper impact?

Reflecting on the first chapter of Mark's gospel, the pope calls us to an imitation of the first and model evangelizer, Jesus. For Jesus, evangelization was essentially a proclamation of the Kingdom or Reign of God, and an articulation of the cost of Kingdom living: conversion. "The time has come," Jesus proclaims, "and the Kingdom of God is close at hand. Repent, and believe the Good News" (Mark 1:15). We will return to the themes of the Kingdom and conversion later.

In paragraph 14 of *Evangelii Nuntiandi*, Paul VI clearly states, "The Church exists to evangelize." In this statement he reminds his readers of two things: (1) Evangelization is the central mission of the Church. (2) The Church was born of the evangelizing mission of Jesus and the early Church. The Church, then, resulted from an evangelical mission and now has a similar mission. This mission is to bring the Good News to "all strata of humanity . . .

transforming humanity from within and making it new" (paragraph 18). It is obvious that evangelization, in the strict sense of that term, is much more than an educational ministry. Evangelization includes all the pastoral activity of the Church in an effort to give birth to a new age and a new world. Evangelization, the pope says, is a complex process made up of many and varied ministries and ministers.

The essential content of evangelization—sometimes proclaimed, sometimes expressed in a life of witness, sometimes communicated in a ministerial moment—is as follows, according to Paul VI:

- The Father's love as foundational for our lives
- Salvation through Jesus
- The promise of eternal life
- The interplay of the gospel and concrete life, an explicit message about liberation from famine, chronic disease, illiteracy, poverty, and other forces of evil
- The need for liberation also from sin
- The final goal of all human beings: happiness in God

Paul VI goes on to list the primary methods of doing evangelization. These include the following:

- *Witnessing.* He speaks of witnessing as the most powerful teaching strategy.
- *Preaching.* He speaks of preaching as a sharing of faith and an act of love.
- *Catechesis* (religious education). Systematic religious instruction—at church, in schools, and in Christian homes—should lead to patterns of Christian living, not just notional faith or a kind of cultural Catholicism. Such catechesis must be addressed not just to children but also to other age groups, using a variety of means.
- *Media.* As the Church learns to employ well the tools of the mass media, the truth of the gospel will be shared in an inestimably increasing way. The Church needs to learn how to use these powerful means.
- *Person-to-person contact.* Basic to effective sharing of the Good News is a personal encounter with a person of faith.
- *The intercommunication of Word and Sacrament.* The Church's preaching and teaching leads to sacraments which intensify the experience of evangelization. Sacraments, in turn, lead to living the values of the gospel (paragraph 48).
- *Popular piety and devotion.* Paul VI speaks of "well-oriented" devotion and popular piety as rich in values and holding great potential for facilitating the work of evangelization.

In chapter five of *Evangelii Nuntiandi,* the pope mentions the *beneficiaries* of evangelization. We might, in American pragmatic culture, speak of the "target groups" for our evangelizing activity.

- *The whole world.*   This beneficiary might seem too broad to be possible; but, in fact, the pope is reorienting the vision of the Church. The Church exists for the whole world. Evangelization is not so much getting people into churches as it is the Church moving out to the world to effect its transformation from within. The Church has been commissioned by Jesus, recorded by Mark, Matthew, Luke, Acts, John, and Paul, for a universal mission. We are not just the chosen people of God; we are light, salt, and leaven for the world.

- *First proclamation to those far off.*   Through a variety of strategies, the Church must engage in a kind of preevangelization effort to those who have never known the Lord. The pope speaks of a renewed proclamation to a de-Christianized world. Included in those "far off" and those de-Christianized, besides those who have never heard of the Lord, are those who have been baptized but have never experienced evangelization or conversion, and also the many people who are involved in non-Christian religions.

- *The nonpracticing.*   Secularization, hurt, and the handing on of religious apathy have created an ever-expanding subgroup that the pope refers to as "the nonpracticing." He mentions that this group is particularly resistant to evangelization.

- *Supporting active believers.*   Including both active Catholics and active Christians of other denominations, the Church needs to support those active in their faith, as they struggle to be believers in a world hostile to faith.

- *Nonbelievers.*   While building on the truth and beauty of various cultures, the Church's evangelizing efforts must be resistant to the forces of secular humanism, which has begun to seep into the various world cultures, creating a kind of universal atheistic culture. The unchurched and nonbelieving are obvious targets for evangelizing.

The pope closes this section with a summary admonition that we evangelize the multitudes. With some caution and exceptions, he points out small-base faith communities as both a means to evangelize those in the small groups and a way to gradually evangelize the larger church or parish.

In discussing the workers of evangelization, Paul VI spends considerable time calling for a delicate balance between the development of strong local churches and episcopal conferences and national identities, and the bond of loyalty, fidelity, and communion that such local expressions need to have with the universal Church. There can be a rich unity between the local and universal Church. The universal Church is the unfolding of the Lord's plan for the Kingdom to come over the whole world.

Within this universal perspective, there are many workers or ministers of evangelization: Peter's successor, bishops, priests, deacons, religious, the laity, the family. Paul VI makes special mention of the young: young people must become more and more the evangelizers to their peers. Indeed the breadth and depth of the Church's universal mission demands *diversified ministries,* which include serious and qualitative formation and training.

In chapter seven of *Evangelii Nuntiandi,* Paul VI reminds his readers of the centrality of the Holy Spirit in the work of evangelization. Strategies and techniques for evangelizing are secondary to the movement of the Holy Spirit, with whom ministers cooperate and for whom ministers serve as instruments. The Spirit is "the soul" of the Church, "the agent of evangelization and conversion," and "the goal" of the Church's evangelizing efforts. The Holy Spirit is the source of evangelization. We who seek to evangelize need to attend to, cooperate with, and minister in and through the Holy Spirit.

In the same chapter, the pope speaks of the centrality of witness in evangelizing. Words about faith are sterile and empty if not joined to actions and behaviors that incarnate the values of the Kingdom. In an age that calls out for authenticity, authentic witness of lifestyle is perhaps our most effective tool. The only religious educators that are listened to with seriousness are those who join witness to words. In both words and witness, the evangelizer seeks to bring the truth of God to contemporary situations and relationships.

Evangelization is prompted by love—love of God and love of those evangelized. The evangelizer has a paternal-maternal love for those in his or her care. Part of loving those evangelized is the practice of a profound respect for their spiritual and religious backgrounds, practices, and sensitivities. Evangelization need not bulldoze people's religious practices or ethical convictions. Evangelization should accept people where they are, affirm their goodness, and companion them into an ever deeper appropriation of the gospel. The evangelization process must include a sensitivity to people's devotional practices, affirming the evangelical potential present in them. The love of the evangelizer includes also a concern for Christian unity. The pope portrays true evangelization as oriented toward the reunification of the Body of Christ. His comments stand as a critique of many popular evangelical movements that are militantly anti-Catholic and also critical of other mainline Christian churches.

The encyclical closes with an admonition to evangelizers to avoid burnout (or in some cases, rust-out), or what Paul VI calls a "lack of fervor." Evangelization is the *duty* of the baptized. It is important for evangelization to be characterized by a joyful spirit. This also critiques many Christians and ministers who undermine any evangelistic efforts that they are engaged in by the joyless attitude that frequently accompanies it. The pope refers to Mary as the "star" of evangelization, entrusting the Church's future evangelizing efforts to her prayer and intercession. (The encyclical was released on December 8, 1975, on the feast of the Immaculate Conception.)

The pope's final reference is to Pentecost, the day that inaugurated the Church's evangelizing efforts. It is obvious that Paul VI was calling for a new Pentecost as we approach the third millennium of Christianity. This new Pentecost will be characterized by the Church consciously reclaiming evangelization as its central mission, or its "basic feature."

RELIGIOUS EDUCATION LED THE WAY

This chapter would be incomplete without mentioning the little-known or now forgotten work in the religious education community that really paved the way for the synod of 1974, the bishops' document, and the 1975 encyclical. Two educators in particular, Pierre-Andre Liégé and Alfonso Nebreda, contributed toward an emphasis on evangelization. In 1954, Liégé, who taught in Paris, wrote an article titled "Evangelisation" in *Catholicisme: Hier, Aujourd'hui, Demain,* in which he distinguished between the steps or stages of *evangelization* and *catechesis.* While *catechesis* refers to the whole process of handing over the Word and tradition, Liégé felt that *evangelization* referred to a first step in the process. The step is one of awakening faith and facilitating initial conversion and metanoia. The problem facing religious education, according to Liégé, is that of *baptized unevangelized Catholics.* Such people have been initiated, and many have gone on to receive religious education or catechesis. They have not, however, experienced personal conversion, or heard a personal call to live the gospel. Without a conscious effort at evangelizing, we have thus mass-produced *cultural Catholics* and *unconverted Christians.* Liégé further felt that the most effective force for evangelization was the community itself. By not just speaking the Word, but also by dramatically and prophetically living the Word, vibrant communities ought to reach out to and attract people who hunger for a similar conversion and lifestyle.

Alfonso Nebreda, who taught at the East Asian Pastoral Institute in Manila, developed a seminal notion of Liégé's, that of preevangelization. By preevangelization, Liégé and Nebreda referred to the relational ministry, tending to needs and wounds, and to the transforming of social structures or oppressive situations that often are necessary as *preliminaries,* before the gospel can be either proclaimed or appropriated. Liégé and Nebreda discouraged any sort of evangelizing style or strategy that might be coercive or manipulative. We need to scrutinize some current efforts at popular evangelism through the filter of this insight. In the 1974 and 1975 documents on evangelization, another of Liégé and Nebreda's principles is developed: that evangelization always needs to be adapted to local customs, culture, and devotion. In *Kerygma in Crisis* and other writings in the 1960s, Nebreda went on to popularize these ideas and the process steps of preevangelization, evangelization, and catechesis.

In the late 1960s, the religious education community began to speak of the need to "historicize" the gospel, or to add to word and witness real efforts at human liberation to round out the mission to evangelize. Some of the documents of the Second Vatican Council articulate this vision, chief among them *Lumen Gentium, Gaudium et Spes,* and *Ad Gentes.* The "liberation" theme and others of Liégé and Nebreda's insights also rinse through *The General Catechetical Directory* (1971), the United States bishops' *To Teach As Jesus Did* (1972), and the U.S. Catechetical Directory, *Sharing the Light of Faith* (1977).

DO WE NEED A NEW WORD?

While speaking to a group of clergy recently, I noticed obvious discomfort on the part of some of the priests whenever I used the word *evangelization,* and especially when I reminded them of Paul VI's vision that evangelization is at the center of what we are about as Church. Several of them rather vociferously shared their disdain for the word *evangelization,* arguing that it is a Protestant word, one that makes Catholic people uncomfortable. Do we use synonyms for evangelization? I do not think so. The word belongs to the entire Body of Christ, Protestant and Catholic. What has happened, at least in American culture, is that it has been "owned" by fundamentalists and evangelicals. They have given the word *evangelization* some connotations or accompanying attitudes that indeed many Catholics and mainline Protestants are uncomfortable with.

It is my preference to use the word *evangelization*, sharing with people the rich insights into all that *evangelization* means, from the bishops, Paul VI, and ancient and recent history. Such a practice will lead many more Christians to reclaim the word and its meaning, and to accept evangelization as both their baptismal right and duty.

A WORD WITH MANY CONNOTATIONS

The word *evangelization* triggers many feelings and thoughts when people hear it. Many people immediately think of *religious education*. For such people, evangelization is the act of *awakening faith*. Catechesis goes on to give awakened faith deeper *understanding*. Some may go on to systematically study faith in the form of *theology*. This is a very acceptable (and common) approach to evangelization. Other people think of *social justice* when they hear the word *evangelization*. Paul VI, as we saw, wrote that evangelization is incomplete if it does not contribute toward the development and liberation of people. Many others think of the Church's *missionary activities* around the world when they focus on evangelization. Another very legitimate model is evangelization as *outreach to the unchurched and inactive*.

In this book, two approaches to evangelization are especially emphasized. The first is *foundational evangelization*. This term refers to the basic proclamation of Jesus as Lord, and an invitation to people to turn from sin and illusion to become more grounded in God. Father Don Kimball, a nationally recognized expert in youth ministry, feels that the largest group of adolescents in need of the Church's attention is composed of *baptized unevangelized* young people. In effect, such youth have had the water of Baptism poured over them, and many have even attended parochial school or CCD. Consciously living as a disciple of Christ, however, is not a value to them. Jesus, for such young people, is simply not the *foundation* of their lives. Other things, people, fads, and values are. I would like to apply Kimball's concern to Catholics and Christians beyond the adolescent stage of life. Among all the various ages and stages of people who call themselves Christians, there is a high incidence of *baptized unevangelized* people.

A question that surfaces at many of my talks around the country is, If foundational evangelization is so important, how do you do it? I resist directly answering that question, because I fear "cookie-cutter" approaches to evangelization. I prefer parishes, schools, and institutions retrieving foundational evangelization as a value, and then strategizing as to how to include foundational evangelization into parish programs and ministries.

The second approach to evangelization that is emphasized in this book has been called by some *convergence evangelization.* This convergence model has been especially propagated by The National Council for Catholic Evangelization, founded in 1983. To understand this approach, I attempt a diagram of the way many dioceses and parishes function.

Religious Education Ministries	Liturgical Ministries	Youth Ministries

Services and Justice Ministries	Financial and Administration Services

The individual boxes above speak of *compartmentalization*— different ministers in different ministries "doing their thing," but not communicating or collaborating with people who are involved in other types of ministries, or who possess different gifts. Too often on diocesan and parish levels, such compartmentalization leads to turfism or people fighting to maintain their kingdoms, but not really harnessing energies for the coming of the Kingdom of God. Compartmentalized ministers and ministries are lacking in shared vision. They go about the *what* of their given ministries, but do not share a common *why* for ministry.

The convergence model challenges dioceses and parishes to get serious about implementing Paul VI's vision, that evangelization is the central mission of the Church. Convergence evangelization can be diagramed as shown at the top of the following page.

The convergence model of evangelization postulates that evangelization is a thread that runs through all of the Church's efforts. Evangelization is the *why* for our ministries. No matter what ministry we might be involved in, all ministries ought to be evangelistic. Education proclaims the Good News; liturgy celebrates it. Pastoral care and justice ministries extend the Good

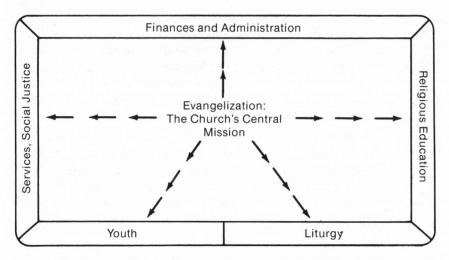

News to those who are wounded or suffering. Finances and administration focus on responsible stewardship and organization for the propagation of the Good News. Evangelization, in the healthy, wholistic sense spoken of by the late pope, cannot really happen unless all ministries (including "nonchurchy" ministries, such as witnessing in the work world) find *the* central mission around which we all must converge—the evangelization of the modern world.

WHY CHURCH?

The Church does not and should not exist as an end unto itself. The Church exists to continue the evangelizing activity of Jesus. Paul VI speaks of a "New Pentecost" for evangelization in his 1975 encyclical. If we want to glimpse what a new Pentecost would look like, we should look at the dynamics of the first Pentecost. In the Acts of the Apostles, Luke paints a picture of a group of anxious, diffident disciples who were not quite sure what to do after the resurrection and ascension of Jesus. The Lucan account highlights three aspects of the first Pentecost.

1. There was an awakening to and cooperation with the Holy Spirit.

2. The experience of the Holy Spirit prompted Peter to evangelize, to preach to thousands.

3. Peter's evangelization prompted the multitude of listeners to repent, to celebrate that repentance in sacrament (Baptism), and to form into communities of prayer, Eucharist, mercy, ministry, and justice. The first Pentecost, then, was an experience that could be diagramed thus:

> *The Holy Spirit* prompted *evangelization*
> and
> *evangelization* begot the *Church.*

There is no Church without evangelizing. Evangelization is the centerpiece of the ministry of Jesus. Peter's evangelizing gave birth to the Church—evangelizing begets Church. In some parishes or communities, there are only cardboard facades of Church, because attention to the Holy Spirit and authentic evangelizing are absent.

We are growing in a new consciousness of Church. The Church exists to continue Jesus' evangelizing activity. The Church exists for the world—to heal and transform the world. The Church exists to help realize the Kingdom or Reign of God; the Kingdom was Jesus' metaphorical reference for the new vision and lifestyle to which He called people. So when we evangelize, we are doing much more than proselytizing for the Church. The Church evangelizes toward the Kingdom of God. And the Kingdom of God is a much bigger reality than the Church.

ATTITUDES AND STRATEGIES

Evangelization cannot and should not be forced into some quick and easy programmatic molds. Evangelization is first an *attitude.* The attitude of evangelization is something that many parishes sorely lack. The evangelizing attitude is one of *invitation* and *mission.* If we study the evangelizing style of Jesus, we discover that His approach is always one of invitation and mission. The hard-sell, manipulative strategies of some modern evangelists are quite far from the scriptural portraits of Jesus' evangelization. Jesus *invited.* When the invitation was accepted, He discipled those who came to Him and then sent those *discipled* on *mission,* the mission of the Kingdom, the Reign of God. Something curious has happened to mainline Christianity. The mainline churches seem to have lost this evangelizing attitude. Father Alvin Illig, director of the Paulist National Evangelization Association, estimates that less than 2 percent of a typical Catholic congregation have an evangelizing attitude.

The fastest growing churches in America are evangelical churches. Specifically, the Assembly of God churches are the most rapidly growing. One outstanding characteristic of these churches is their evangelizing attitude. This attitude is certainly one of *mission.* Fundamentalist, evangelical churches see the world—the marketplace—as the real arena for evangelizing. While mainline Protestant and Catholic churches evangelize those who come to their buildings, these evangelical churches move out into the neighborhoods and the work place to evangelize. The parish or church that has lost this attitude of invitation and mission has become incestuous, closed in upon itself, or maintenance oriented, concerned with maintaining the status quo.

Evangelizing attitudes do not necessarily accomplish a great deal. And so, evangelizing attitudes need to be wedded to serious attempts at *strategizing.* Strategy refers to goal setting, program planning, and program implementation. I fear that we are experiencing a crisis of creativity in many local parishes. Author Tom Peters, in both *In Search of Excellence* and *A Passion for Excellence,* writes about the importance of innovation in developing successful business. *Innovation* is a word that, in principle, needs to be applied to evangelization. Mainline churches do not often reward innovation in evangelizing. In a world rapidly changing in terms of communication techniques, we will be terribly unfaithful to our mission if we do not develop a more innovative approach to strategizing for evangelization.

It is important to highlight the balance needed between an evangelizing attitude and evangelizing strategies. American parishes and churches, reflecting American pragmatism, often reach for the program or strategy. Why is it that parishes can employ programs of renewal for months or years, and yet they remain essentially unrenewed? It is because such communities jumped for the strategies or the program without an ecclesial or community conversion to the attitude of evangelization, that is, an attitude of invitation and mission.

INVITATION AND MISSION:
For What?

As mentioned earlier, Catholics and mainline Protestants often have negative feelings about the word *evangelization* because they intuitively connect it with the "evangelical hard sell." For just a brief space, let us review two principles that are crucial in these evangelical groups: *maximum influence* and *multiplication.* Maxi-

mum influence is rooted in the theology of Matthew, chapter 5, in which Jesus encourages disciples to be light and salt for the world. Maximum influence reminds Christian communities that they do not exist for themselves but rather as agents of change and influence for the world around them. *Multiplication* is oriented toward mission. Disciples go on to disciple others. Evangelical Christianity uses the familial terms of *spiritual parenting* and *grandparenting* to express the multiplication principle. Multiplication simply refers to the process of disciples handing on the gift of faith, meaning, and Christian wisdom that they have received. Those who have been gifted with faith go on to multiply disciples by giving as gift what they have received as a gift.

Maximum influence and multiplication are healthy concepts that come from evangelical Christianity. They are practical strategies that incarnate the principles of *invitation* and *mission*.

It is time for us to look at the theological-spiritual realities that undergird all thinking or conversation about evangelizing.

THE KINGDOM OF GOD

Paul VI wrote that the essence of what evangelization is about is contained in one scriptural verse, Mark 1:15: "The Kingdom of God is close at hand. Repent, and believe the Good News." The Kingdom of God was at the root of what Jesus was about in His evangelization and ministry. The Pharisees and other Jews were often confused by what He meant by the Kingdom, Jesus' most frequently repeated theme. As did most Jews of the time, many of Jesus' hearers thought of the promised Reign of God in geographical, time, and space terms. But when Jesus spoke of the Kingdom, He was speaking more of a new perception of life. The Kingdom of God is first of all a vision of life. The vision consists of beginning to see life and experiences as Jesus did.

A prayerful study of Scripture reveals the following as key to the new life vision of Jesus. Kingdom people experience life as "shot through" with the presence and influence of God. God is experienced as alive and involved in the human story and experience. The God experience is summed up by the word *Abba*. *Abba* is the word used by Jesus to express His relationship with the Father. *Abba* connotes special warmth, love, and intimacy that is possible with this loving God-parent. The regal overtones of Jesus' Kingdom vision were especially appropriate for the people of what we now call Israel and the Middle East. Israel was accustomed to being overtaken and occupied by foreign powers and its own leadership or monarchy subjected to exile and alienation. *Kingdom* or *Reign* were symbols that spoke of dominance. The *Kingdom of God* refers to Jesus' conviction that only God can be foundational for life. Idolatry, on the other hand, was and is an attempt to build one's life on fragile, nonultimate foundations. Kingdom people realize that there is one foundation for life: the love, Spirit, and influence of God. Belief in the presence of God's unconditional love leads people to other Kingdom attitudes: trust, vigilance about the quality of life, prayerfulness, and a paschal spirit that senses new life coming from obstacles, pain, and death.

The Reign of God is more, however, than well-intentioned attitudes. The Kingdom is a *lifestyle*, lived in time and place, *in community.* The Kingdom of God needs to take flesh, form, reality in concrete behaviors and ways of living. Jesus preached and taught the Kingdom, but He also embodied the Kingdom in His works of charity, healing, and justice. Paul VI reminds us in *Evangelii Nuntiandi* that evangelization certainly involves words, but the most authentic evangelization is frequently found in wordless witness, that is, a lifestyle that embodies the attitudes and values of the Kingdom. People who have decided for the Kingdom realize a responsibility for the transformation of the world. Each Kingdom person, in however small a way, plays a role in the redemption of society, and in reorienting the world toward the plan and will of God.

CONVERSION

As we saw in Mark 1:15, Jesus speaks of the price for Kingdom living. It is *conversion.* "Change your lives," He proclaims in His invitation to believe the Good News of God's closeness and availability. Conversion is a complex phenomenon that includes decisions, changed behavior patterns, and a faith-rooted interpretation of human experience. Most people need to experience change on at least three levels of life for true conversion to the Kingdom. First of all, most of us develop a kind of private or inner logic that is often flawed by mistaken notions about life's meaning as well as by sin. This private logic often is at variance with the values of the Kingdom of God. Similarly, on the second level, society tends to develop a kind of corporate logic. The corporate logic of modern Western society is characterized by consumerism and materialism, which offer the security of acquiring, accumulating, and possessing things. Contained within the life visions of consumerism and materialism are a devaluing of the person, a valuing of power and aggression, an overemphasis on self-gratification, and a depreciation of sexuality, personal commitment, and relationships. Obviously, true conversion must penetrate not only private logic but also the misguided common sense of the culture. Finally, on the third level, genuine conversion lifts us beyond the limits of organized religion to experience genuine spirituality, specifically the spirituality of Jesus. Conversion is a going above and beyond religion to spirituality.

While some people can point to single events of conversion, times in which their lives were literally turned around, conversion is more often a process, a movement that we appreciate in hindsight. Nonetheless, conversion necessitates the conscious decision making of a person, away from mistaken notions and sin and toward the truth of the Kingdom. The number and types of human experiences that can function as conversion thresholds are unlimited: falling in love, falling out of love, psychological struggle, relational ups and downs, moral and intellectual pursuits. Usually conversion involves the presence and influence of a person or people of faith in the life of the converting person to help him or her find God present in human experience. The absence of such faith influences can lead to the opposite reaction of losing sight of or belief in God.

A parish interested in evangelizing realizes that it exists for the Kingdom. A parish that is Kingdom oriented knows also that its chief responsibility is to create an environment in which conversion is enabled and facilitated. Human beings do not make conversion happen. Rather, we are vehicles or instruments through which the Holy Spirit, the agent of conversion, works.

DISCIPLESHIP

If Paul VI stressed Mark 1:15 as a scriptural foundation for evangelizing, evangelical Christianity places similar emphasis on Matthew 28:17-20. Called by evangelicals the "great commissioning," this passage contains a picture of Jesus mandating apostles and disciples to go into the world and make *disciples*. Evangelization always involves the making of disciples.

We cannot fully appreciate what discipleship is without an analysis of the Jewish rabbinic tradition of discipleship. In the interactions between rabbis and disciples, the appropriation of doctrine or content was secondary to the development of the rabbi-disciple relationship. Jesus' style of discipling especially emphasized relationship with Him as teacher and the acquiring of His values. The scriptural portraits of discipleship present disciples as on a journey, pursuing a personal relationship with Jesus, appropriating His values, and continuing His mission.

To evangelize is to invite to the Kingdom, facilitate conversion, and make disciples.

CONCLUSION

This chapter has been an attempt to articulate a vision of evangelization. We proceed now to explore, in the subsequent chapters, practical considerations for parish evangelization. Specifically, we will look at the evangelization of active church members, inactive and alienated Christians, the unchurched, and youth. These four beneficiaries, or target populations, received significant attention in *Evangelii Nuntiandi*.

2

Evangelizing Active Parishioners

With great wisdom Paul VI reminded the readers of *Evangelii Nuntiandi* that the Church must be in a constant state of evangelizing itself. The only way that a parish has anything to offer, the only way that a parish can evangelize alienated and/or unchurched people, is by making ongoing attempts at individual and communal conversion among active parishioners. In this chapter, we will explore eight general areas that parish staff and parish leaders need to attend to, in an ongoing way, to better create an environment of spiritual renewal and conversion.

BEWARE OF PROGRAMITIS!

Theologian Richard McBrien, in a recent article, complimented the *Renew* program, which began in Newark, New Jersey, and has expanded its influence to national and international dimensions. McBrien says that *Renew* is probably the best parish renewal program available. But he adds that unfortunately, in some parishes, *Renew* does not accomplish the goal of in-depth parish renewal. The reason, he says, is that true renewal requires long, hard work in many aspects of parish life that *Renew* does not touch—issues like parish structures, development of lay leadership, parish decision making, prayer, and worship.

I share McBrien's perception of the parish renewal scene. Many fine programs for renewal are now available. But paradoxically, some parishes can be deeply immersed in renewal programs and at the same time sidestep genuine renewal. *Programitis* is a term I have coined to describe the tendency of some parishes to rush to the newest programs on the market, and then stack those programs one on top of the other. Programitis creates a chaotic, busy parish, but it does not spark an innovative, organic generation of renewal processes that flow from the parishioners and staff themselves. If prepackaged renewal programs have any value, it is to serve as sort of "training wheels" on a bicycle. Just as the training wheels exist to help teach a young child to ride the bicycle, the parish renewal program exists to teach the parish how to plan, organize, and program creatively, using the gifts and resources of the parishioners themselves. The eight constants for renewal that are described in this chapter represent areas of parish life that need consistent fine tuning through "home-grown" parish creativity and effort.

CONSTANT ONE:
Renewal of Parish Vision

Too often parishes are reactive organisms. They move when touched, or respond to crises. But they are not proactive in the sense of having a corporate identity, with an eagerness to take the initiative in the evangelization of society. The parish will remain reactive rather than proactive if it is not challenged to face the identity issue, or to ask and answer the question, Who are we as a people of faith at this time, in this unique place? The real problem in this reactive vs. proactive tension is *not* that parishioners are lacking in vision. Everyone who is considered "active" in faith has some sort of a vision or outlook on God, Jesus, Church, and parish. Unfortunately people hold on to their individual visions without ever joining resources in articulating a communal or corporate vision. Implicit in our individual vision of parish are expectations, principles, and theologies. Because they are never surfaced, named, and talked about, much misunderstanding, hurt, anger, or conflict can arise among parishioners and between parishioners and staff. In talking about a renewal of parish vision, I am referring to the need of parishes to engage in a process of articulating a vision statement of parish.

A vision, or mission, statement is a statement of the purpose, or reason for existence, of a local parish. It should be noted that vision statements change according to the racial, ethnic, socio-economic, and geographic makeup of the community. No two parishes ought to have the same vision statement. The method of arriving at a vision statement needs to be *process* in nature. The process ought to be participative, or as inclusive of as many parishioners as possible. The process of arriving at a vision statement is often as important as the vision statement itself. There are several strategic ways of beginning the renewal of parish vision.

Developing a Vision Statement

In resourcing parishes around the country on this primary level of parish renewal, I usually begin with the parish staff. Quite often, misunderstanding and mistrust can be present among these, the leaders of the parish, because they have never shared on the level of vision and theology of parish. Questions that can begin to facilitate sharing in an initial staff meeting are *Why should this parish exist?* and *What are the theological or spiritual principles out of which I operate in my ministry to this parish?* Enough time should be given for some reflective writing on these questions. After naming feelings and thoughts in writing, the staff can move on to begin sharing. It is important to have a nonstaff facilitator who can objectively guide this process along. What should especially be highlighted by the facilitator are the areas of agreement among participants' visions, as well as unique contributions that each vision offers to the group. This first meeting should conclude with the surfacing of one or two editors from the staff, who will take the most significant sharing and try to unite the visions in a nonrepetitive block of prose. The staff has, in effect, begun to articulate a parish vision.

But the vision statement will remain irrelevant for most of the parishioners if they are not brought into the process. The staff needs to take their seminal work out to the parish organizations, and engage the various parish groups—from boards to ministering groups to organizations—in a process similar to the one in which the staff engaged. After each such meeting, an editorial team, now with parish members, must add new insights from the meetings. Care needs to be taken to avoid repetition and a forced, wooden style of composition.

As parish groups are involved in the process, attention needs to be given to those parishioners who do not belong to any parish organizations. Their input also needs to be solicited. In some cases, parishioners will not want to be involved in the process. However, it is important that the invitations at least be extended. Sunday homilies and bulletin articles, for example, could invite parishioners at large to a "town hall" meeting to explore their vision of parish. Again an editorial team needs to be creative in building their input into the statement.

One discipline that an editorial team needs to place on itself is to be parsimonious in words, to avoid verbosity. Once the editorial team and staff feel the process is complete, the vision statement needs to be officially promulgated. Some parishes have done this liturgically, at a Sunday Eucharist. The parish vision statement is unveiled and then installed in a highly visible place in the parish church. The parish has described itself, taken upon itself a renewed sense of identity. It is now ready to consciously engage in the mission of evangelization.

It should be noted that the parish or vision statement needs to be looked at again and again over the years in order to evaluate it, to reshape it, to keep it fresh. This statement must always reflect the fluid and changing nature of culture, neighborhood, needs, theology, and spirituality.

Complementary Strategies for a Renewal of Vision

While articulating a vision statement remains an important step in renewing a parish's way of seeing and understanding itself, it is not the only way. Many dioceses around the United States have begun to dust off an old tool: the parish mission, often called "the revival" in the black community. Hispanics have also begun to gather in auditoriums and stadiums for large group "event evangelization." The mission, revival, or event—through music, song, and ritual—is better able to offer substantive preaching, theology, and spiritual renewal than the homily at Sunday Eucharist permits. In reality many Catholics need "new thoughts" about their own faith lives and membership in their Church and parish. The prayerful celebrative contexts of these religious experiences provide a rich environment for this sharing to take place.

The notion of a mission might generate negative feelings in many who connect the word with the fire-and-brimstone preaching that they experienced in childhood or adolescence. Many of us who have begun again the work of parish missions operate out of much different strategies. If a parish requests a mission, I spend some time interviewing the staff and parish leaders. We discuss details about the nature and style of the mission. The real life needs of the local community are especially analyzed. For example, a parish in the steel mills section of Chicago requested a mission. As some readers might know, significant portions of the steel industry have abandoned the city of Chicago. Parishes on the far east side of Chicago are emotionally, spiritually, and economically depressed. Divorce is on the rise. Male alcoholism is increasing at an alarming rate. The mission for this parish had to "fit" the needs and wounds of that community. The gospel had to speak to that unique situation, just as a mission would similarly have to fit a different set of needs in an economically sound community.

Bringing the gospel to bear on the existential situation of people through heartfelt preaching and religious experience can begin the renewal of a community's vision. The attraction that many Catholics feel toward evangelical churches and the messages of TV evangelists is, in part, a hunger and thirst for religious experience. The mission, revival, and event can satisfy some of that need—all in the context of Catholic culture.

Usually the vision statement process and such religious experiences as the mission, revival, or event are parallel or complementary efforts. In both strategies people need to hear about four gospel realities that often get buried in the busyness of parish life. The nature of the Kingdom of God, personal and communal conversion, discipleship, and mission to the world must be central to a parish's vision.

CONSTANT TWO:
Renewed Priorities

As parishioners grow in identity and a sense of mission, certain issues of parish life surface as real priorities for the parish in its responsibility to evangelize. Some of these "priority items," and comments on their relevance for parish evangelization, are listed in this section.

Need Discernment

In an ongoing way, parish staffs and leaders need to keep an ear to the ground relative to parish needs. Too often parishes jump to do programs rather than fashioning programs around perceived needs. Recalling Liégé and Nebrada's insights, we must keep in mind that some people need a kind of preevangelization, or ministry to aches and wounds in their lives, before they can really appropriate the gospel. Sometimes the most effective evangelization is done by bringing the gospel to bear on real life needs. Evangelization efforts, targeted on needs, seek to accept people where they are, and build on real life situations.

Need discernment can be done in a variety of ways. Some parishes use instruments like the sample survey on pages 28–29 to tap the needs of those who attend Sunday Eucharist. Time can be given after the homily for people to complete the survey. The results can be tabulated, and goals and programs should flow from the results of the survey.

A SURVEY OF ADULT RELIGIOUS CONCERNS

In your opinion, which of the following topics are important enough to you to warrant inclusion in our Adult Program? Please check as many as you think are important.

☐ Church-state relations
☐ Legalizing abortion
☐ Divorce
☐ Drugs/addictions
☐ Suburban living/urban living: problems and tensions
☐ Medical ethics
☐ Adolescence and problems of faith
☐ Church history
☐ Catholic and non-Catholic relations
☐ Future of Chrisitianity
☐ Changing priest/sister
☐ Changing Church
☐ Business ethics
☐ Birth control
☐ Changing role of lay people in the Church
☐ Why Catholic education?
☐ Christian in the modern world
☐ Freedom and authority in the Church
☐ Prayer and Devotions
☐ Applying Christian principles to daily living
☐ Conscience: rights/responsibilities
☐ Censorship in mass media (TV, radio, movies, books)
☐ Why am I Catholic?
☐ Bible study groups and "get acquainted" courses in the Old and New Testaments
☐ Capital punishment
☐ Married life/relationships/family
☐ Exploring other religions
☐ Personal development workshops
☐ Other:_____
☐ Other:_____

Are there any obstacles that would prevent you from participating in Adult Programs? Please list in order of importance.
☐ Babysitters
☐ Disinterest in Adult Programs
☐ Lack of information about the programs
☐ Lack of transportation
☐ Times at which the activities are scheduled
☐ Other:_____

FACTUAL DATA

SEX: ☐ Male   ☐ Female
AGE GROUP:
  ☐ High School ☐ 18–25
  ☐ 26–35   ☐ 36–45
  ☐ 46–55   ☐ 56–over
MARITAL STATUS:
  ☐ Single   ☐ Married
  ☐ Widow   ☐ Widower
  ☐ Separated   ☐ Divorced

Please indicate the two most convenient times for you to attend/participate in an Adult Program. Number your choices 1 and 2.

Weekdays	Weekends
_____ Morning	_____ Morning
_____ Afternoon	_____ Afternoon
_____ Evening	_____ Evening

Please number in order of preference the three most appealing formats for programs to be presented.

_____ Film or slide presentations

_____ Lectures

_____ Panel discussions

_____ Lectures followed by questions and answers

_____ Informal group discussions

_____ Workshops

_____ Lectures followed by small group discussion

_____ Other: _____

Suppose this line represents your involvement with your parish church. Please circle the number that you think represents where you are (1 is the most involved and 6, the least).

| 1 | 2 | 3 | 4 | 5 | 6 |

Since our last survey, we have tried to fulfill your wishes concerning what Adult Christian Enrichment should offer. We discovered six general areas of concern. The following statements are evaluations that you can make about each of the general areas. Please put the number of the statement that you feel applies next to each general area listed below.

1. I would still like to hear a lot more about this area.
2. This area is no longer applicable to me and my circumstances.
3. This area has been very well covered and needs no more coverage for a while.
4. I was very satisfied with this area and the way it was covered.
5. I am dissatisfied with the way this area was covered.

GENERAL AREAS

_____ Self-understanding, Self-help
_____ Family Life, Parenting, Marriage Relationships
_____ Awareness of Social Issues, Addiction, Stealing, Justice
_____ Conscience Formation, Rights and Responsibilities, Human Life, Morality
_____ Contemporary Church, Changes in the Church, Liturgy, Authority
_____ Prayer and Spiritual Life, Personal Prayer, Eucharist, Contemplation

If you have gone to any of our programs, we would sincerely appreciate your comments on the helpfulness of each one as well as the failings.

Program _____

Comments _____

Program _____

Comments _____

Are there any issues that you wish to be presented that are not included in this survey? Are there any general areas you wish to be discussed?

_____

_____

We would appreciate having your name, address, and phone number, if you wish to give us this information.

Name_____

Address_____

_____ Phone _____

Names and ages of children: _____

_____

Thank you for your cooperation and patience in filling out this survey!

In addition to surveys, parish town hall meetings can be quite helpful in allowing parishioners to share about areas of need and concern in the community. Home visitation, to which significant attention is given in Chapter 3, is also effective in giving parish leaders a sense of what is going on in parishioners' lives.

Only after need discernment has taken place should parish leaders become involved in generating programs. The logical sequence is (1) need discernment, (2) goal setting, (3) pastoral planning and program design, (4) time lining program implementation, (5) sharing responsibility for the program pieces, and (6) making provision for evaluation.

A Mission Statement for Each Organization and Ministry

We have already looked at the importance of a process that helps a parish arrive at a mission statement. The same process needs to be engaged in by each parish organization and ministry. A dilemma that often occurs in parish life is that programs and organizations continue to function from year to year, and the people involved in them literally forget why they were begun. Parish programs lose a sense of identity and purpose. After a parish has articulated a mission statement for the entire parish, each parish group should engage in a similar process, resulting in an identity and mission statement for each parish group. This statement should name the group's unique mission and show how it fits in with the larger mission of the entire parish.

Focus on Adults

In Chapter 1, we discussed the nature of discipleship from a scriptural perspective. A common denominator among the disciples who walked with Jesus was the fact that they were adults. Parochial schools and child-centered CCD programs continue to be "the tail that wags the dog" in many communities. Jesus played with children and formed the adults. We reverse the process, playing with adults and evangelizing children. Building on discerned needs, the parish should reach out to adults with educational and pastoral care efforts. In many of the parishes that I have resourced there are recurring needs that give rise to excellent opportunities for the evangelization of adults. These needs include marriage enrichment, parenting adolescents, the stages of adult development, and coping with stress and depression. The National Advisory Committee on Adult Religious Education, of the U.S. Catholic Conference Education Department, issued a statement in October 1985, outlining three main goals of adult religious education: (1) to help individuals and communities understand and live the gospel, (2) to help adults exercise a prophetic voice in the world, and (3) to help adults share their faith with the next generation.

Family-Based Religious Education

Much has changed in American culture. One of the most obvious changes is in the style of family living. One out of three marriages ends in divorce. One out of two attempted second marriages similarly ends in divorce. Single-parent families and blended families are significant subgroups in the typical parish. In addition to these trends in marriage and family life, the fabric of American society, the context for marriage and family, has also experienced major shifts. Twenty to thirty years ago, the neighborhood, the Church, and both public and parochial school systems all mutually supported each other in handing on a shared value system. Cultural, ethnic, and moral pluralism has multiplied in America, resulting in a breakdown of this educational ecology. Though the educational ecology has broken down, we still attempt to do religious education with basically the same techniques we used decades ago—namely, the "schooling model" of both parochial schools and CCD programs.

In the schooling model, religious education focuses on children but allows parents to remain largely uninvolved in the process. The most involvement that some parents have in the religious education of their children is driving them to school or CCD. What we have wandered into is a style of doing religious education that, in effect, mass produces the inactive Catholic. Inactive parents are not challenged to break out of their inactivity. Religious education becomes a curious thing for the children in such families. The message of the classroom seems irrelevant to or incongruent with the family lifestyle to which they return. "If this is not so important to Mom and Dad," many children must wonder, "why should it be important to me?" The style of religious education becomes a louder message than the words of the catechist. The message is too often that God, Church, and spirituality are boring and dull.

Curricula need to be redesigned so that on a regular basis mothers and fathers from both school and CCD efforts engage in a family experience with their children. One model that I have designed for several parishes includes monthly family liturgies for every grade level of religious education, seasonal celebrations of reconciliation for families, and suggestions for home activities based on themes the children are studying. In addition, the staffs of the parishes involved sit down with all the parents of school and CCD children to discuss the importance of a covenant bond between home, the religious education department, and parish staff in fulfilling the parish's mission to evangelize.

In a recent address to family life ministers, Bishop Howard Hubbard, ordinary of Albany, New York, called for everyone involved in ministry in today's parishes to develop a "family perspective" in designing all parish programs. He referred to a "family lens" that educators, liturgists, pastoral care ministers, and youth ministers need to apply to both program planning and evaluation. In short, Bishop Hubbard advocated the vision of John Paul II in *Familiaris Consortio*, that the family (in the varying shapes and forms it now appears) is the domestic Church, the target of parish evangelizing efforts, and, in turn, the Church's most important evangelizing tool.

"Journey" Sacramental Programs

In a wonderful book on renewing Catholic sacramental life (*The Book of Sacramental Basics*), author Tad Guzie encourages parish leaders to add a process similar to the process of the catechumenate to each sacramental preparation program in the parish. For those unfamiliar with the process of the catechumenate, let us briefly review its main features.

The catechumenate, or Rite of Christian Initiation of Adults (RCIA), as it is also commonly called, has its roots in the early centuries of Christianity. Those seeking entrance into the Christian community engaged in a step-by-step journey toward the Sacraments of Initiation. Those steps included an evangelization period, an education period, a time for discipling and proximate preparation for the sacraments, the sacramental celebration, and follow-up ministries after the celebration. A number of ministers facilitated this whole process: ministers of the Word (education and formation), ministers of prayer and worship, and guidance ministers. A fourth ministering force was the Sunday assembly, with whom the candidates interacted, prayed, and celebrated. The Eucharistic community was aware of and involved with the candidates for sacraments.

In resourcing parishes on how to make sacramental celebration more truly evangelistic, I try to apply some of the above ideas to restrategizing for sacramental preparation. Rather than intellectual experiences, sacramental preparation sessions should follow that journey motif of the RCIA, including periods of evangelization, catechesis, proximate preparation, and follow-up ministries. New ministries are needed that are similar to the guidance and discernment ministry of the sponsor. As much as possible, especially with first Eucharist and first Reconciliation, the family ought to be looked on as the candidate for the sacrament, not just the child. Candidates and their families ought to regularly be present at one of the Sunday masses. Finally, the sacramental moment should not be looked on as a graduation or termination. Parish ministers in sponsorlike roles ought to do follow-up work with individuals or families who have celebrated sacraments. The following letter reflects the efforts of one parish to help develop a family consciousness to religious education and the journey motif of religious education and sacramental preparation. You may wish to send a similar letter to the parents of children in your programs.

Dear Parents and Guardians,

Thank you for participating in our parent information and consultation evenings. For parents who were unable to attend we hope to meet with you as soon as possible.

The steps in our "Emmaus" Family Religious Education Program and in our Family Sacramental Program, as well as the dates of the family masses for each program, are listed below.

I. "Emmaus" Family Religious Education Program

For people involved in our elementary program at St. John's Parochial School and School of Religion (CCD), grades 1 through 8, the following experiences are held:

A. *Classroom Sessions.*   Each young person attends religion class to grow in his or her Catholic Christian faith.

B. *Family Activity Sessions.*   Once a month, each young person will bring home an activity to discuss with you. The young people will be asked to share their experience when they come back for their next religious education session.

   NOTE: We ask you to try to spend some time with each child. When that becomes difficult, as it often does in larger families, take the assignment of one of your children and involve your other children in that activity. The other children can report back in class about that particular activity even if it was not their assignment.

C. *Family Masses.*   Families are encouraged to participate once a month in the family masses held in church. The masses will be planned by parents and where possible will include the children and young people as ministers. The schedule for masses for families with children in Parochial School and in School of Religion is as follows. Note that at the 11:00 A.M. mass on Sunday, May 11, the families of children in primary, intermediate, and junior high grades will worship together.

11:00 A.M. SUNDAY FAMILY MASS

	Oct.	Nov.	Dec.	Jan.	Feb.	March	April	May
Primary	27	10	15	12	9	9	13	11
Intermediate	27	24	15	26	23	9	27	11
Junior High								11

5:30 P.M. SATURDAY FAMILY MASS

	Oct.	Nov.	Dec.	Jan.	Feb.	March	April
Junior High	19	16	7	18	15	15	19

NOTE:

1. Once the mass is over, you may return home. There is no meeting with your child in the school after mass.

2. Since our Family Sacramental Program will be held on some of the Sundays on which there will also be either a primary or an intermediate family mass, families whose child is involved in a sacramental session are asked to attend the family Eucharist or Reconciliation mass at 9:30 A.M.

3. There will be two opportunities for families to participate in the Sacrament of Reconciliation. One will be in Advent, the other in Lent. You will be notified of dates and times as soon as possible.

II. Family Sacramental Program

Children in grade 2 will be asked to participate in the Eucharist Program, and children in grade 4 will be invited to participate in the Reconciliation Program. This is in addition to their regular classroom sessions.

A. *Requirement.*   Children must be in a school or school of religion program one year before they are accepted into the Family Sacramental Program. Children in grades 3 through 6 who have never received the Sacrament of Eucharist or the Sacrament of Reconciliation would be included in the Family Sacramental Program. Although these children would attend the 9:30 mass with their parents, they would learn with children on their own grade level at other times.

B. *Dates and Times.*   Below are the dates of the Family Sacramental Program. The program begins with the 9:30 A.M. mass. Parents and children will come to school after the mass for learning as well as working on a family activity. The session will end by noon.

	Oct.	Nov.	Jan.	Feb.	March	April
Eucharist	13	10	12	9	9	13
Reconciliation	27	24	26	23	23	

It is our hope that you do not see this emphasis on the family as a burden on you or your child. We pray that these programs might encourage all of us to learn and pray, to talk and share feelings, to build up our own individual families of St. John's.

Improving Liturgy and Religious Experience

In a book entitled *Why People Join the Church*, author Edward Rauff isolated four ingredients that contribute to the development of a *magnet parish*, or a parish that people are attracted to and attend without consideration of geographic boundaries. Those four ingredients are:

- programs that respond to genuine needs,
- liturgies that provide some form of religious experience,
- preaching that offers a livable spirituality, and
- congregations that communicate warmth and hospitality.

The importance of tending to needs, the first ingredient, has already been discussed. The next three of Rauff's indicators are all focused on the Sunday liturgy. The importance of Rauff's insights lies in his emphasis on the Sunday celebration as the parish activity that quantitatively touches the most people among those who are active in church attendance. The issue for those of us interested in evangelization is, Can we also begin to touch people *qualitatively* through liturgy and preaching?

In Chapter 3, on ministry to the inactive, I share some insights from the neurolinguistic school of psychology. Neurolinguistic research stresses that people take in and put out communication on three channels: auditory, visual, and kinesthetic. Most people develop a dominant channel and a back-up channel, but leave one channel underdeveloped. I might be, for example, a person who is visual-kinesthetic dominant, but weak in the auditory area. People with an auditory orientation have a great capacity for listening, and are comfortable with *ideas*. Visual people need to see things; they even image scenes as they read novels. Visual people are intrigued by *stories*. Kinesthetic people tend to communicate and take in communication on the level of *feelings* or *emotions*.

I summarize this material briefly because I think it has great value and relevance for the preacher. Any preacher who simply preaches from his or her dominance will lose two-thirds of the congregation. The effective homily touches people on all three channels: auditory, visual, and kinesthetic. The effective preacher shares *ideas* and *stories*, and arouses *feelings*. Such was the preaching and teaching style of Jesus. Preachers-to-be as well as those already engaged in such ministry need a great deal of input and practice in the skills of effective communication. A good homily:

- triggers a counterexperience in the listeners as they realize similar experiences have happened to them,
- brings Scripture to bear on human experience, highlighting the God-presence in human experience,

- shares faith through human experience,
- moves listeners toward a hint or intuition of the mystery of the Incarnation, helping them realize that God is close, real, involved, and available, and
- leads listeners to take some sort of action toward realizing and actualizing the Kingdom.

When there is talk of improving liturgy, the conversation naturally turns to the clergy. But Rauff's indicators remind us that liturgy is truly "the work of the people." The congregation needs to be reminded of its role in making liturgy a truly evangelistic experience. Catholic privatism and anonymity still negatively affect liturgies around the country. Too many people still come to "eat their own supper," rather than to join in communal prayer and celebration. If there is such a thing as presidential style, there certainly also must be such a thing as congregational style. Congregational style refers to the quality of singing, presence, and participation at liturgy, as well as such courtesies as arriving on time and not leaving early.

Parish expert Father Philip Murnion, from New York City, says that the word that best describes the style of participation in parish by Catholics of the future is *voluntary*. Rather than being swept along by guilt or obligation, Catholics will *choose* to join or not to join in worship. Research done by Abraham Maslow, years ago, indicated that people want to be in groups in which they feel esteemed, wanted, and important. Murnion's and Maslow's insights converge in my own mind as I reflect on liturgy and evangelization. Catholics are choosing, and will choose with greater frequency, to celebrate in congregations in which there is warmth and hospitality displayed by the community.

Social Justice Consciousness

The evangelizing mission of the parish must be joined to activities intended to liberate people and transform society. This connection between evangelization and social justice rinses through Paul VI's *Evangelii Nuntiandi*. Karl Barth used to say that the preacher who is true to the gospel always preaches with a Bible in one hand and the newspaper in the other. The preaching and teaching function of the Church must transcend the boundaries of personal, privatized salvation. Preaching and teaching must consciously engage in *conscientization*, or helping believers develop their consciousness concerning the justice issues of our day: racism, sexism, the threat of nuclear war, poverty, hunger, and other issues. Conscientization refers to that internal networking of judging, evaluating, and deciding relative to the morality or immorality of situations, conditions, attitudes, and behavior. The notion of *conscience* needs to be expanded in Catholic culture to include societal and global concerns.

Related to conscientization is *politicization*. Too often Christian people of all ages accept the status quo of life. We take life as it comes to us, often misused and misshaped by the demonic forces of the culture around us. Politicization refers to people awakening to the reality that indeed we can shape reality and the future. Politicization involves putting the values of the gospel into action. Both conscientization and politicization are attempts to incarnate the Kingdom in a time, a place, and a people rather than leaving it unrealized and unactualized, in poetry and theology.

In this line of thinking, social justice consciousness and activity are constitutive to evangelization and religious education. Religious education is interwoven with the quest to change reality. In our day, Paulo Freire, author of *Pedagogy of the Oppressed* (1972), and Thomas Groome, author of *Christian Religious Education* (1982), have been advocates of this style of education.

Pastoral Care Ministries

Religious educator Dr. Parker Palmer writes and speaks on the unique ministering style of Jesus. Jesus certainly evangelized through the spoken word, but He also evangelized through His healing activities. The healing touch of Jesus was an incarnation in time and space of God's healing, unconditional love. This healing love was and is especially directed to the wounded and broken. A parish committed to continue the evangelizing style of Jesus needs to continue His mission of healing. The parish's mission to heal can take shape in a variety of ways:

- Training ministers of care for the hospitalized, shut-in, or those in nursing homes
- Developing support groups for widows, widowers, and others who are grieving; the divorced, single parents; and children of divorce
- Allowing independent self-help groups to use the parish facilities: Alcoholics Anonymous, Alanon, Alateen, Narcotics Anonymous, Families Anonymous, Tough Love
- Hiring pastoral counselors whose full-time ministry is to be available for guidance, counsel, or spiritual direction

These are but a few suggestions for a parish interested in becoming a healing force in the community. Recalling the convergence model of evangelization (pages 15–16), it is important for us to keep in mind that evangelization can happen not just through educational ministries, but through all of the Church's ministries, specifically through healing ministries.

The Role of Women

As hierarchy focuses on the issue of the role of women in the Church, it is also important for this issue to be consciously addressed on the level of parish life. Psychologist Rudolf Dreikurs wrote years ago that the greatest revolution awaiting us is one that leads to the equality of the sexes. As feminism and women's rights continue to accelerate on the American business and cultural scenes, we as Church run the risk of an increasing lack of credibility if we do not promote justice in this area, as other institutions do.

Evangelizing in the Context of Racial and Ethnic Pluralism

For years, the American parish could be administered with a "cookie-cutter" approach. There were a certain number of organizations and sacramental services that a parish was expected to deliver. But contemporary parishes are much more complex organisms than those of previous decades. In addition to the different styles of families present in American parishes, many parishes, especially those in cities, are also a rich racial and ethnic mix.

Hispanics now constitute one-third of the American Catholic population. Chicago sociologist William McCready maintains, however, that 30 to 40 percent of Hispanic Catholics are not involved in parish life. Because of a void of Hispanic leadership in the American Catholic Church, because also of a failure on the part of many parishes to provide services, education, and worship bilingually, many Hispanic Catholics find the American Catholic parish a strange, unfriendly environment. This "failure of omission" on the part of the Catholic Church has resulted in both an aggressive attempt on the part of non-Catholic religions to evangelize and proselytize, and a significant number of Hispanic Catholics crossing over to other denominations. The United States bishops' pastoral, *The Hispanic Presence: Challenge and Commitment* (December 12, 1983) has called for new and creative attempts to minister to Hispanic Catholics.

Chicago is but one of many centers of Catholicism and Hispanic presence that is trying to respond to the bishops' challenge and this ever-growing opportunity for evangelization. In an expansive effort entitled *Para Servirle* ("At Your Service"), we have trained close to seven hundred home visitation ministers who serve as bridges of reconciliation between local parishes and the families and individuals in various neighborhoods. There is a parallel effort made with the staffs of these Hispanic parishes to help in their ongoing formation and training for evangelization.

Only 1.2 million blacks, out of the total national black population of 25 million, are Roman Catholics. The black challenge to Catholic evangelization is not the "drain off" problem of Hispanics. Rather it is, Do we as a church have anything to offer black Christians? Research into the experience of blacks in the American Catholic Church shows that parishes did not readily welcome blacks, and forced them to establish their own parishes or to sit in restricted portions of white churches.

A renewal of Catholic evangelization in the black community necessitates improved outreach through the Rite of Christian Initiation of Adults, improved catechetical programs and pastoral care services, and better liturgy that gives expression to emotional, deeply felt black spirituality. The black community can also benefit from the home-to-home visitation efforts described in several sections of this book.

Chicago has also attempted a special effort in the area of black evangelization. In the more than eighty parishes that are largely black in the Archdiocese, black Catholics gathered to study and talk about the implications of *Evangelii Nuntiandi*. Similar gatherings were held for the black bishops' pastoral *What We Have Seen and Heard*. Several hundred have been trained in skills for home visitation. An Archdiocesan revival attracted two thousand people nightly to Holy Name Cathedral. Regional centers have been established for quality adult education.

These unique needs of and renewed strategies for Hispanic and black evangelization are paralleled in many other subpopulations in American parishes: the Filipino, Korean, Vietnamese, Italian, Polish, and many other communities.

A Rebirth of Youth Evangelization

I consider this topic of such vital importance that I place it among the agenda items of a parish in renewal, as well as dedicate an entire chapter of this book to a serious study of it. We have a great deal to learn from Protestants and evangelicals, who for years have given much more attention, funds, and personnel to developing creative models of evangelizing youth. I will mention just one model in this section, that is, *organic growth youth ministry.*

Evangelical youth movements very consciously focus on the possibilities of discipleship and conversion in the life of young people. One of their strategies is to gradually build a youth program that grows naturally and organically. The strategy looks like this:

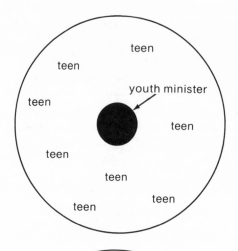

1. The youth minister begins on a small scale, discipling a small group of teen leaders.

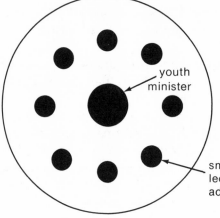

2. Those who once were in the central circle with the youth minister reach out and form their own small faith communities. Trained adults and young adults guide and support these peer ministers.

small faith communities led by peer ministers and adult/young adult advisors

3. The youth minister, adult and young adult mentors or advisors, peer ministers, and young people in their small communities reach out to those young people who are not too connected with the community. These unchurched or disconnected young people are consistently called and contacted by mail, inviting them to the social and formational events of the youth program. Ongoing outreach is also extended to them, to invite them into the small groups or to other recreational, educational, or retreat opportunities.

Two principles, previously discussed on pages 18–19, guide this ever-expanding strategy for youth evangelization. The first is *maximum influence.* Maximum influence speaks of the responsibility that youth movements and communities have to reach out to and touch as many young people in a given area as possible. The second principle, *multiplication,* captures the true evangelical nature of forming disciples. A young disciple ought to grow to the point of reaching beyond the self to help the process of discipleship begin in someone else's life.

More on the challenge of youth evangelization can be found in Chapter 4.

These eleven priority items are issues that I hear recurring over and over in the planning of parishes who have taken that first step of renewing a sense of vision and mission. It should be noted that to attempt all of them at once would result in paralysis. Parish leadership, after completing the process of articulating a mission statement, can study these issues, possibly generate other priorities, and then engage in setting goals and in time lining to achieve these goals.

CONSTANT THREE:
Renewal of Parish Through Small Faith-Sharing Groups

In their recent book *How to Save the Catholic Church,* Andrew Greeley and Mary Greeley Durkin speak of the importance of generating organic communities within the larger parish context. Rather than the experience of programs and structures being imposed from on high, organic communities are small groups of believers that naturally cluster together for a variety of reasons. Gradually the association and meetings of these people take on the identity of a community.

About seven years ago, something began to trouble me about Chicago Catholic parishes. In our large parishes we were using lots of Vatican II jargon about *community* and the *people of God,* but the fact was (and still is) that many people did not know each other in the parish. In fact, people could be living across the street from each other for years and never say hello, have a conversation, or share in any meaning. While my firsthand experience was in large suburban communities, ministers in urban parishes concurred with my perception that a crippling syndrome for evangelization and community formation is *Catholic anonymity.*

Sociologists have written over the last decade about the decline of the neighborhood, as many of us experienced it as we grew up. Tightly knit communities of relatives and friends, living in close proximity to each other, sharing commonly held values, were common experiences in the turn-of-the-century immigrant parishes. This phenomenon perdured through the thirties, forties, and fifties. But the exodus to the suburbs that began in the sixties dramatically altered the nature of parish life. The new parishes that developed in the suburbs became loose associations of people who were transplanted from their roots. The post-Vatican II ministries that developed in many parishes dispensed catechetical, liturgical, and sacramental services. Many of these ministries, however, left people locked in anonymity and in their private spirituality rather than helping them "become community."

Though researchers see a new rise in a concern for relational bonding in neighborhoods, the experience of the last twenty-five years has been isolation and alienation. In terms of parish, much of the potential membership in most parishes has remained what Father Tom Sweetser calls, in *Successful Parishes,* "active uninvolved." "Active uninvolved" refers to people who attend mass but do not become involved or invested in the activities and ministries of the community. In addition to the "active uninvolved" syndrome, the rise in alienation from the Church, in which large numbers of Catholics "dropped out" from involvement in the parish, has become a real source of concern for the parish in recent years. The decline of neighborhood consciousness, the nomadic nature of American families, individuals pulling up roots recurrently for job-related reasons, and other alienating forces have created, in many cases, parishes that *talked* about community but had no existential experience of community.

Since 1978, I have worked part-time as a consultant in two parishes. In both parishes, I have worked with staff and parishioners in creating a neighborhood ministry project. These efforts have not been clear-cut, clearly programmed successes. They have been rambling, expansive efforts, with some loose structuring and organization, heavily dependent on parishioners "owning" the ministry (leading, administering, and serving). In other words, no program manuals or flow charts were used. Operating out of the basic structure and organization that parishioners helped to develop, each area of the two parishes decided the number and nature of activities that would help their area.

In the first pilot parish, neighborhood ministry began with a six-week Lenten program. Beginning well in advance of Lent, the parish staff sifted through the parish files in an attempt to contact a number of people whom they knew well. These people were sent a personal invitation regarding the Lenten program. This approach was an attempt to build a success factor into the project through personal invitation, as well as an attempt to attract new leaders who were dedicated to parish life but had not yet found a niche in parish ministries. A general invitation was also extended to the parish at large. The publicity stressed that the Lenten program was an attempt to take a hard look at the quality and the identity of the parish, its strengths, and its weaknesses. The goal of the staff was to work with parishioners around the question: How can this parish become more truly a community?

Close to 250 people attended the initial meetings. These numbers thinned down to about 150 by the end of Lent. When they came to the sessions, the people were seated in clusters of seats set apart by placards indicating the seven regions of the parish in which they lived. People from the same region sat together. Thus the evenings together, at least in environment, resembled minipolitical conventions. On each of the evenings the groups focused on a different theme of parish life, using small group discussion, large group processing, and some input. Topics included the following:

1. Fond memories that people had of Catholic parish life

2. How the Church changed in the past twenty years

3. The needs that the people of the parish perceived

4. New ministries that would target newly perceived needs

5. The concept of minicommunities or neighborhoods

Items 3 and 5 went "hand in glove" for those of us who had seen the need to confront the impersonal tone of the parish. In the need discernment, a frequently articulated need was the need for greater sharing, friendliness, and community in the parish. The people who engaged in the Lenten program proposed a neighborhood ministry pilot as a way of finding a solution to the anonymity problem.

Leaders, people with deep interest in the project, emerged throughout the Lenten process. Also, the group process surfaced what people felt a need for in the smaller communities: adult education and Scripture study, liturgy and social experiences. Eventually, the equivalent of a "lay vicar" was discerned for each of the seven main regions. Each region was broken down into small cells. In the smaller cells, leaders were sought for the following ministries, which tended to the above-mentioned needs:

1. Coordinators for block and backyard parties

2. Coordinators for small group discussion and education

3. Coordinators for home masses

4. Coordinators for the welcoming of new parishioners

Each of the cells was not able to surface leaders for each of the ministries; thus some of the ministries were done on a scale larger than a cell (several blocks within a region).

The project worked with much enthusiasm for many people for several years. A change of staff, however, brought in new full-time staff members who were not interested in that style of parish. If I had stayed on, I would have developed further what had begun as a subproject of the neighborhood ministry program, that is, the gradual transformation of the children's religious education program into a more family-based, neighborhood-oriented process. Clusters of parents began to assume responsibility for the catechesis of their own and each other's families. A new parish in the suburbs of Chicago is beginning its religious education efforts on such a model right from the start. Without a "mainstreaming" of the neighborhood or small group model into the programs and processes of the parish, neighborhood ministry can become "just another program" that the "elite" might participate in. The bulk of the parish, however, remains in status quo parochial programs and impersonal parish life.

In trying to adapt my first experience to another assignment, I met with some resistance. The second parish was quite different from the previously mentioned parish, which was attempting to live the vision of Vatican II. The second parish was quite conservative and had a devotional style. Efforts at small group adult education or even socials were not appealing to people. Noticing an Eastern European man kneeling before a large statue of Mary one day prompted me to try something. During Advent, an empty manger, handmade by a carpenter in the parish, was passed from home to home for either prayer services or home masses. The theme celebrated was "Let Jesus be reborn in our hearts." A similar process was engaged in during Lent, around the central symbol of a cross that was passed from home to home. Three things were accomplished in these religious experiences in the home: (1) neighbors were invited into each other's homes; (2) adult formation was experienced in dialogue homilies; (3) social time with refreshments followed the religious experience. If there was a weakness, it was that, at least in the beginning, the process was rather priest-dependent. But such was the nature of the parish. Leaders that emerged in this effort went on in the next two and one-half years to become leaders of *Renew,* and the *Renew* program became the agenda of the small communities. The small groups are now going on to use the *Parish Spirituality* series produced by the Office for Chicago Catholic Evangelization.

Another parish that I am currently resourcing is being divided into subareas, and each of its six deacons will serve as pastoral coordinator of one area, with a variety of ministers working in the area under the leadership of the deacon and his wife.

St. Louis, Missouri, in concluding the *Renew* program, encouraged parishes to be creative about the continuation and nurturance of small groups. People can form small faith-sharing groups around criteria other than neighborhood or geographic proximity. A common ministry in the parish, a common problem, special interests, parenting, marriage, divorce, the single life, and so on, are all types of common denominators around which people can form small groups.

St. Joseph's Parish in New Hope, Minnesota, has moved much of its pastoral ministries onto the regional level. Ministry to the sick, adult education, and other efforts are all coordinated in subregions.

Father Alphonsus Navarro, director of S.I.N.E. (Sistem-Integral-de-Evangelicion), has a strategy for the formation of base communities, which he both uses as a pastor and teaches as director of his organization. Base communities are a staple of life in this process: to belong to the parish is to be in a base community. First, however, individuals and/or families must have a "foundational evangelization" experience, wherein Jesus Christ as Lord is both proclaimed and appropriated. Father Navarro uses a variety of techniques for this evangelization—from courses to seminars to retreats. Only after evangelization can membership in a small community make sense.

For anyone interested in beginning to develop small faith communities, two resources are helpful: Stephen Clark's *Building Christian Communities* (Ave Maria Press, 1972) and Edward Braxton's *The Wisdom Community* (Paulist Press, 1980). Clark says that if small communities are going to develop, some of the following conditions are necessary:

1. Group members must have a real commitment to each other.

2. The group must meet regularly.

3. Participants must be geographically close enough to each other to be able to meet without great difficulty.

4. The focus of each group must be a conscious attending to and sharing of faith.

Braxton's book adds the importance of common reading materials to stimulate the thinking and discussion of group members.

John R. Welsh, S.J., in an article entitled "Comunidades Eclesiais de Base: A New Way to Be Church," in the February 8, 1986, issue of *America* magazine, describes two types of base communities that are popular in Latin America. One is the mini-parish model, similar to my neighborhood ministry model. In this model, the ministries of the parish are offered in the microcosm of small geographic communities that make up the larger parish. The other is the family group model, in which several families meet for prayer, Scripture, and reflection on life situations. Father Thomas Kleissler, co-founder of the Renew movement, has been advocating a rethinking of the parish as a *community of communities.* The small communities that would make up such a parish would be characterized by prayer, life sharing, support, and outreach. Kleissler goes so far as to say the role of the pastor is to train parishioners to become co-pastors in the small communities.

CONSTANT FOUR:
Renewal of Ministry

In his excellent book *Theology of Ministry,* Thomas O'Meara challenges his readers to look at ministry through the eyes of early Christians. Too often ministry on the parish level is equated with tasks, the staff doing tasks as well as soliciting parishioners to do tasks. Such an approach is quite far from the experience of the early Church. Ministry was not an add-on responsibility for a few—a few activists taking on the tasks of the community. Rather, ministry was a responsibility that flowed from Baptism. In fact, everyone ministered. The ministry that a disciple engaged in was determined by both the needs of the community and the gifts and charisms of the baptized individual. O'Meara's challenge is to retrieve that original reality of "ministry according to charism."

In one parish in which I work as a consultant, the staff had a Ministry Sunday—a fairly common reality now in which liturgies and homilies focus on the ministerial needs of the parish. After a general presentation on ministry, people who felt or heard a call to ministry were asked to submit their names on cards. They could also indicate if they felt a leaning toward any particular ministry:

education, youth, worship, finances, administration, or pastoral care. For the next month, the staff held discernment sessions on each of the major areas of ministry, explaining the nature of the ministry and also explaining the charisms or gifts of the Holy Spirit. Prayerful time was then given to each person to discern what his or her particular charisms might be. The people were encouraged to begin thinking about making a commitment to an area in which they felt they were gifted or had charisms. This initial process took place in the post-Pentecost season, drawing from that season the theme of mission. The summer months were then spent in School of Ministry sessions for each major ministerial division. The staff offered some of the sessions; for other sessions, outside facilitators were brought in. This particular parish uses the seasons of Advent and Lent for adult education around discerned needs and also small faith-sharing groups, and the winter months are given over again to additional School of Ministry sessions.

Although the above process does not function as smoothly as it sounds on paper, I believe this approach to parish ministry is a healthier, more integral direction than the approach that calls people to tasks. More on ministry, specifically how to structure for "parishioner ministry," is presented in the next section. I also believe we need to clarify for the people of God that ministries need not always be seen through the filter of the parish program, or as something being done at the parish plant. Jesus speaks of disciples as servants who minister subtly in their world, acting as salt, light, and leaven. This involves living gospel values at work, in the neighborhood, and in the family. One's gifts of the Spirit ought to be used in and for the world, not just for the parish program.

Some parishes have developed a unique approach to ministry. In addition to the marketplace ministry just described, some parishes are attempting to network people in similar or parallel situations of struggle. Those who have lost a child are connected with parents who have already lived through that struggle. Those suffering from anxiety or depression are put in touch with people who have the same kinds of difficulties. The unemployed minister to each other, and on and on. The pastor or some other credible, trusted figure must serve as the conduit through which such information is shared and connections made. In all cases, confidentiality must be respected.

We cannot leave this discussion of ministry without looking briefly at the issue of leadership. Two dynamics are present in the contemporary Church: the explosion of baptismal, or lay, ministry, and the decline of vocations to the priesthood. The priesthood seems to have fallen into a severe identity crisis. Young men are not attracted to a job description that is increasingly diffuse in nature or a lifestyle that includes mandatory celibacy. All of this raises questions about the style of leadership that priests in general and pastors especially should utilize.

The pastor of the contemporary parish and his staff need to become like orchestra leaders, bringing the gifts of many people to blend together into something beautiful and better than the gifts and people operating in isolation. No ministry should begin in a parish unless parishioners are available both to lead in administering the ministry and to do the ministry. The parish and staff are enablers and empowerers. Not only does the pastor need to encourage the many people coming forward for parish ministry, but he must also be the spark plug and source of encouragement for his staff. The pastor often has to back away from the immediate gratification of being the direct dispenser of parish services, and become the coach who prods and encourages others in ministry. Tom Peters has written about this style of leadership in his books *In Search of Excellence* and *A Passion for Excellence*. He speaks of true leadership in terms divorced from power images. For Peters, the true leader is a coach-type person who has a dynamic vision of what could be, who is servant of those with whom he works, and who enables and empowers them to use their gifts and talents. A good leader, a good pastor, encourages innovation and entrepreneurship among his or her workers. Through a ministry of presence, or by "wandering around," he or she becomes an ongoing source of nurturance for those ministering in the community.

CONSTANT FIVE:
Renewal of Parish Structures

In his recent best-seller *Megatrends*, John Naisbitt mentions a number of major trends that he perceives to be changing the social and economic landscape of America. Among them are (1) the South is replacing the North as the economic and business hub of America; (2) high technology is awakening in many people a need for "high touch," or intimacy; and (3) "either or" thinking is being replaced by "multiple option" thinking. The trend that struck me the most was this one: hierarchies are being replaced by networking. The importance of networking, or linking, ministers and ministries for evangelization cannot be overemphasized. One area of diocesan and parish life that needs to be under careful scrutiny and reshaping is *structuring*. If the Kingdom is to be more fully realized, diocesan and parish structuring needs to move more and more toward the networking or linking of various ministries, offices, and departments in a common dedication to the cause of evangelization. Failure to unite for the Kingdom creates toxic turf fights and a multiplication of efforts involved in trying to preserve one's own ministerial kingdom.

Father Jim Dunning, our nation's bright pastoral light on the RCIA, speaks frequently about the new wineskins needed for the new wine of the RCIA. The RCIA is so revolutionary in intent that some traditional parish structures and attitudes simply do not provide a fitting or nurturing context or environment. The RCIA demands new wineskins. So it is with evangelization. Traditional ways of organizing or structuring dioceses or people can impede the mission of evangelization rather than facilitating and expanding it. Often parish and diocesan structures mirror each other. Diocesan offices speak a message of noncooperation, or lack of vision, and parishes reiterate the message in their planning and structuring.

This book is an attempt to propagate a convergence model of evangelization. There is an area of Christian living on which all the ministries of a diocese or parish converge. I believe that midpoint to be evangelization. All diocesan and parish efforts should contribute to the one central mission of inviting people to the Kingdom of God and a conversion-discipleship stance in living. After dioceses and parishes have had this primary awakening—that indeed all offices, boards, groups, and individuals should have a common vision anchored in evangelization—then people can proceed together to seek common-sense structures that will facilitate all involved in their unique contribution toward evangelization.

Key in effective structuring is networking, or linking. While "hierarchy" will be a perduring metaphor for our Church, that approach needs to be wedded to a healthy networking of diocesan agencies and parish groups. Such an approach both respects the authority of bishops, priests, and trained ministerial professionals, and at the same time redefines such leadership in terms of enabling or empowering others for evangelization. Hierarchy is not the obstacle to evangelization in Catholic practice; the obstacle is often the result of a larger systemic situation. I am speaking here of a failure to realize the shared evangelistic mission we all have, and flowing from that, a lack of communication (and other strategic failures) that keeps us safely compartmentalized but also estranged from our true mission.

How can we begin or continue to move toward more wholistic strategies for diocesan and parish evangelization? I would like to make a few modest proposals based on my parish, diocesan, and national experience.

Good Clustering

Each diocesan or parish ministry needs a hub, out of which it operates. At the parish level, such a hub might be called a board of ministry. On the diocesan level, it might be called a department. The "bottom line" ministries of the Church that would need a team, or a hub, would seem to be these:

• Ministries of the Word (formation and education)
• Liturgical Ministries
• Service Ministries (including efforts at social justice)
• Youth Ministries (teens through young adulthood)
• Finance and Administration

So, on a parish level, structures might look like this:

Board for Ministries of the Word   Board for Liturgical Ministries
Board for Service Ministries   Board for Youth Ministries
           Board for Finance and Administration

Parishioners' Owning of Leadership

Each parish ministry, anchored in one of the above boards, should be administered by a parishioner leader or couple. In addition to belonging to a board of ministry, each parishioner leader works with a team of ministers for the unique ministry he or she leads. Therefore, board membership might look something like this:

MINISTRIES OF THE WORD
   • DRE
   • Other staff consultants for education
   • Representatives from parochial school
   • Representatives from CCD or its equivalent
   • Parishioner leaders of:
        adult education
        neighborhood faith communities
        RCIA
        evangelization of the inactive Catholic
        marriage preparation
        family first Eucharist preparation
        family first Reconciliation preparation
        baptismal preparation
   • A number of elected members

LITURGICAL MINISTRIES
- Staff resource for liturgy
- Parishioner leaders of:
  - lectors
  - ministers of communion
  - music ministry
  - ushers
  - prayer groups
  - liturgy planners
  - children's and families' liturgies
- A number of elected members

SERVICE MINISTRIES
- Staff resource for service ministries
- Parishioner leaders of:
  - ministry of care to the sick and shut-in
  - ministry to the separated and divorced
  - ministry to the unemployed or impoverished
  - ministry to men
  - ministry to women
  - ministry to widows and widowers
  - ministries toward peace and justice
  - parenting education
  - Alcoholics Anonymous
  - Narcotics Anonymous
  - Families Anonymous
- A number of elected members

YOUTH MINISTRIES
- Staff resource for youth ministry
- Representatives from parochial school junior high catechetics
- Representatives from CCD junior high catechetics
- Adults and youth representing junior high social program
- Adults and youth representing junior high retreat program
- Adults and youth representing high school social program
- Adults and youth representing high school religious education
- Adults and youth representing high school retreat program
- Parishioner leader of Confirmation program
- Parishioner leader of ministry to troubled youth
- Parishioner leaders of young adult ministry
- A number of elected members

FINANCE AND ADMINISTRATION
- Financial consultants to the parish
- Physical plant and maintenance consultants to the parish
- Parish business manager

The chairperson(s) of each of these boards and other needed officers should be discerned among each board's membership. Meeting monthly, each board should rotate its agenda each month to one of three areas: business (decision making, evaluating, program planning), training (in the area of the board's expertise), and faith formation. Each board member is responsible to transfer back to his or her program or ministry group the direction and decisions of the board. In turn, each board member represents his or her program or ministry group to the team. During the months designated for business, each of the ministries represented on the board should be focused on at least once or twice a year in terms of evaluation, decisions, and program planning.

A diagram of the interactions in this strategy would look like this:

---

1. *The staff consultant*
(resources)
a program/ministry leader
(who administers)
a given program or group of ministers.

2. *The program/ministry leader*
(administers)
a given program or group of ministers
(that serves or ministers to)
a given target group in the parish.

3. *The given program or group of ministers*
and the given target group
(are represented on)
a board of ministry
(by)
a program/ministry leader.

Beyond Parish Councils

Parish councils need to break out of legislative stances to facilitate the ministry of the parish and its boards of ministry. The structure of such a council might look like this:

PARISH LEADERSHIP COUNCIL
- A representative from each of the following:
  the Board for Ministries of the Word
  the Board for Liturgical Ministries
  the Board for Service Ministries
  the Board for Youth Ministries
  the Board for Finance and Administration
- The parish professional staff
- Representatives of the small faith-sharing communities and/or geographic divisions of the parish

The functions of the parish leadership council, carried out in cooperation with the pastor, should include (1) evaluating, supervising, and guiding the boards of ministry; (2) long-range planning and visioning for the parish; (3) establishing the focus of spiritual formation for each year.

Beyond Volunteers and Elections

The ordinary process of choosing leaders for various ministries, who also serve as board members, is best done by *discernment*. This involves the staff resource person for a given area of ministry working with the members of a program or ministry team on discerning who among them (or perhaps not yet on the team) would best lead, administer, guide, and represent a given parish effort. If the ministry is just beginning, the discernment of leaders largely has to be done by staff members and those already in parish leadership. Discernment is prayerful discussion, watching, waiting, searching, and deciding. The boards should, in turn, discern who their representatives to the leadership council will be. A parishioner leader should serve in a given leadership position on an average of two to three years, thus assuring a fair and fresh rotation of leadership.

Avoiding Elitism

Joined to discerned leaders on each board could be elected representatives, perhaps three to five for each of the boards of ministry. These elected members are representatives from the parish-at-large, charged with the responsibility of scrutinizing the boards' efforts, as well as being fully involved in the boards' work.

Reaching Out and Expanding Ministries

How do staff and discerned and elected leaders surface lay ministers who will serve in the various ministries of a parish? I have found that it is done best by both one-to-one contact and en-masse invitation. One-to-one contact means that all parish ministers are constantly on the lookout for people who might share in the ministry of the parish. En-masse invitation involves using large group opportunities in the parish to speak of the various needs of the parish and the need for more ministers to come forward to serve.

Matching Charisms with Needs

Such recruitment for ministry needs to be joined to discernment—a prayerful examining of parish needs, of the elements involved in a given ministry, and of the unique charisms of the persons called or invited to ministry. In short, does the person fit the need?

Anchoring in Spirituality

Leadership and ministry ought never to be divorced from spirituality. Ministry that does not flow from growing, deepening spirituality degenerates into flat, burdensome tasks for which people volunteer. Often people do not even understand *why* they are doing the tasks.

Imperative for Good Training

No one should be called to ministry or leadership without the assurance of sufficient training. Considering the busyness of parishioners, training should be sufficient in both quantity and quality, but also not overly taxing on people's time and energy. The boards and council ought to be given some common, basic skills that all ministers use, no matter what the target or focus of ministry might be. Included in these basic skills are need discernment, the articulation of mission statements, the efficient structuring of tasks, communication skills, conflict management skills, program planning and shaping, and evaluation skills. Provision ought to be made also for ongoing resourcing in the areas of Christology, Scripture, ecclesiology, morality, prayer and spirituality, and teaching skills.

How to Do Training

Opportunities for implementing the two preceding items ought to be made available at monthly board and council meetings. In addition, participation in regular on-site formation and education sessions as well as in diocesan-sponsored training should be encouraged. Some parish staffs and leaders around the country have formed their own schools or colleges of ministry, or have networked with other staffs and leaders in area-wide training.

The above suggestions are only hints at a direction for the future based on my work with parishes in Chicago and around the country, as well as my doctoral research. In no way am I suggesting that every parish ought to start all the ministries that I have suggested. Neither am I saying that all of the suggested structures would fit every parish. More important, I believe, are the principles underlying my suggestions. The principles emphasize the unleashing of the power of the laity, the effective networking of parishioners, ministry that flows from spirituality and includes ongoing training, the importance of discernment joined to election, a revised role for the professional staff (enablement and empowerment), and a more common-sense approach to what we have traditionally called parish councils.

CONSTANT SIX:
Renewal of Calendars

Some American parishes have a pagan ritual known as the "yearly calendar meeting." At this meeting, leaders of organizations and parish ministers compete for parish space for their upcoming events. While such events at least keep the use of the parish buildings somewhat coordinated, this gathering hardly constitutes a group of people with a shared vision, creatively planning and programming for the fostering of the Kingdom and the gospel. Often in a parish there are so many calendars that parishioners lose touch with the one main calendar—the liturgical year, the journey toward Easter, the journey of the catechumenate which ought to be the journey of all disciples.

The busyness of contemporary parish life can cause parishioners to lose touch with what ought to be the "aorta" of parish life: the cycles of the liturgical year and the different moods and postures of spiritual life and conversion that it suggests for each of our lives. The liturgical year cannot be truly appreciated if it is seen separate from the movement of the catechumens. Chapter 5 of this book is devoted to special questions about and adaptation of the RCIA, but in this chapter we need to consider the RCIA. Of all current efforts, the RCIA certainly holds within itself the greatest potential to renew parish life.

In what ways can the RCIA renew the parish? First of all, the real ministers of the catechumenal journey are the parishioners themselves. There may be a ministry team that serves in the name of the congregation; but the community, the Body of Christ, actually serves as the facilitators of conversion for the catechumens. Second, especially if proper attention is being given to the liturgical year, the congregation ought to experience itself as being on the very same journey as the catechumens, the journey toward Easter. Third, as the RCIA sinks roots in a parish, many parish efforts can develop catechumenal attitudes and strategies. The principles of the catechumenal process can be applied in various ministries: religious education, sacramental preparation, pastoral care, youth evangelization, and reconciliation with inactive or alienated Catholics. Finally, the presence of cate-chumens in a parish, plus other parish ministries that become catechumenal in nature, challenges the parish to become what it claims to be—the ever-converting Christian community, the Body of Christ.

Some parishes around the country have developed a "cate-chumenal mind-set" about how the parish is to live and grow. As much as possible, "conversion" and "journey" are motifs or metaphors that serve as overlays for the work of the entire parish. Though obviously an oversimplification, a flow chart of such a catechumenal parish might look like the one on pages 58–59.

There are some national experts in the RCIA who rightly warn parishes not to allow the RCIA to be diminished to a pro-gram that runs parallel with the typical parish CCD programs, from September to April. Notice on the RCIA tract, in the dia-gram on pages 58–59, that the strategy I try to implement is a total year effort. *Precatechumenate* and *evangelization* begin for a new group while another group is experiencing *mystagogia*. In the parishes that I resource, in other words, the seasons or movements of the catechumenate are offered yearly. But each person taking the journey is ministered to uniquely. Some choose to take two years to experience the process. Others feel the year is adequate. In catechumenal ministry there is, of necessity, a tension between the *program* and the *process*. A ministerial effort needs some structure to give it shape, form, and identity. The RCIA must have programmatic pieces. But those pieces are tools used in a process that also includes discernment, attention to the individual, and awareness of conversion as a movement of the Holy Spirit.

CONSTANT SEVEN:
Renewal of Tone—Developing a Sense of Mission

Much of what should be considered in this section is covered elsewhere in this book, in the sections dedicated to developing social justice consciousness (pages 36–37) and a ministry of reconciliation to the inactive or alienated member (Chapter 3). Thus, a few comments will suffice here.

The tone of the parish can be represented by two poles on a continuum. Pole one is the tone of maintenance; pole two is the tone of mission. Parishes whose tone leans toward maintenance are basically concerned with the delivery of parish services: sacraments, organizations, some programs. The focus of maintenance-created parishes is always "the self" of the parish. There is little concern for a larger, more expansive concept of possible target groups for ministry.

As is stated elsewhere in the book, the parish ought not to see itself as an end unto itself. The parish, like the larger Church, is a tool—a tool whose purpose it is to help make the Reign of God more and more realized in time and space. The true focus of the parish and the Church and all their efforts is the world, the marketplace, the neighborhoods, the mores of the nation, and the geopolitical climate of the world. The parish's mandate from Jesus to be an agent of reconciliation in the world necessitates the development of a truly inclusive attitude on the part of parishioners. The *Catholic* nature of our faith means that we are not an elite group standing apart from the world, but a catholic, inclusive group that stands for and with the world, but is not necessarily of the world.

Becoming a people with a sense of mission usually requires that quality work has to be done on the other constants listed here. When a parish has seriously tried to engage in self-renewal, it almost naturally begins to reach beyond itself out of concern for the unchurched, the alienated, the downtrodden, and in the direction of the local and global communities.

CONSTANT EIGHT:
Renewal of Individual and Communal Prayer Life

I was asked recently what I consider to be the greatest gift a religious education program could bestow on a person who might be a part of it. I was surprised at my quick, spontaneous reply. I said that the greatest gift that we can give to people in religious education is to teach them how to pray. Prayer is faith expressing itself, faith lived, faith articulated. Prayer is the language of conversion. To the degree one has ceased to pray, or to pray deeply, one also has allowed his or her journey of faith to become superficial or stagnant.

LITURGICAL YEAR:	ADVENT	CHRISTMAS AND ORDINARY TIME
RCIA PROCESS:	*Precatechumenate* • Awakening of faith (begun around Pentecost and continued in summer, fall, and Advent)	*Catechumenate* • Education of faith • Immersion into the community
ADULT RELIGIOUS EDUCATION:	• Need discernment for the coming year • Large group and base community formation on discerned needs	• Ministerial training for those in ministry • Large group and base community adult catechesis
FAMILY SACRAMENTAL PROGRAM:	• General sessions with parents, listening to their needs, questions, hurts—joined to faith experiences with children	• A series of catechetical experiences that blend adult contemporary understanding of sacraments with faith experiences with children
PASTORAL CARE MINISTRIES:	• Relating to the hurting person, either in visitation of the sick, counseling, or any other pastoral care ministry	• Providing the hurting person with resources to begin to perceive suffering from a faith perspective
YOUTH MINISTRY:	• Social experiences • Formation of small youth communities • "Encounter experiences" wherein need for God is perceived	• Ongoing faith formation, based on needs, in nonschooling packaging
ALIENATED CATHOLICS:	• Calling ministry and homecoming events	• Catechumenate-like series in which individuals or families get new information about the Church, have new experiences of Church, and meet new people involved in the parish

LENT	EASTER	EASTER SEASON, PENTECOST, AND ORDINARY TIME
Purification and Enlightenment • Discipleship • Faith deepened and purified	*Sacraments* • Commitment • Vowing	*Mystagogia* • Ongoing development • Precatechumenate begun for a new group
• Parish mission • Large group and base community focus on spirituality	• Holy Thursday, Good Friday, Holy Saturday, and entire Easter season liturgies	• Easter to Pentecost celebration (large group and small group sessions on the paschal mystery, the Spirit, and the missionary dimension of the Church) • Ministry Sunday (calling people to ministry) • Help for those who come forward to discern their gifts for ministry • Training for ministry next fall
• Period of final preparation • Focus on spirituality	• Celebration of the sacrament	• Follow-up ministries after the sacrament
• Helping the hurting person discover a new appreciation of prayer, Scripture, and sacrament	• Facilitating a recommitment to Jesus and the Kingdom amidst pain	• Providing ongoing ministry and relationships with the parish
• Period of discipleship in proximate preparation for Confirmation	• Confirmation • Completion of initiation • Owning one's faith • Owning the mission of the Church	• Ministerial roles in the parish
• Participation in parish Lenten program	• Holy Week and Easter, as celebrations of Reconciliation	• Follow-up ministries (i.e., sponsorship relationships) with those who have returned

In a recent attempt to resource small faith-sharing groups in a number of parishes in the Archdiocese of Chicago, I developed some study materials on styles of prayer. Healing prayer was modeled as a way of inviting the Spirit into unresolved wounds from the past. Centering prayer was experienced as a possible way of penetrating the anxiety and stress that so many of us experience. Prayer that anticipates future events was also modeled, as well as scriptural prayer, prayer of solidarity with those suffering around the world, and journal writing. Many adults who had grown up with the "saying prayers" approach to prayer expressed gratitude at having their prayer lives enriched. The six-week series in multiple parish communities reconvinced me of the value of the teaching style of Jesus when it comes to prayer. Jesus taught people to pray, not through lecturing about prayer, but rather by praying with them.

Parish programs and ministries need to make prayer an obvious, conscious, deliberate priority. Some parishes are trying to do this by scheduling a definite prayer time at each meeting—not just a few seconds, but rather a significant block of time. Some other parishes have structured themselves so that three different styles of meetings are held regularly by various organizations: one month the meeting is totally on business; the next month the agenda is continuing education; the next month the meeting is dedicated solely to prayer together. Other parishes have inaugurated a "parish prayer time." At this time (for example, 6:30 P.M. each evening) individuals and families are encouraged to set aside fifteen minutes for prayer—alone or together. The bulletin is used as a prayer aid.

Mark Searle and David Leege collaborated in 1985 on a study entitled *The Celebration of Liturgy in the Parish.* This study was the fifth report or volume of a larger study, *The Notre Dame Study of Catholic Parish Life,* sponsored by the Institute for Pastoral and Social Ministry and the Center for the Study of Contemporary Society of the University of Notre Dame. In this particular study, the authors report a great deal of unevenness in the implementation of Vatican II's liturgical renewal. Of special importance is the enduring reluctance on the part of American Catholics to genuinely experience and celebrate community at liturgy. The report indicates that among the weaker points in American Catholic liturgy are participation in singing, hospitality at the greeting and other parts of the celebration, and a prayerful understanding of and participation in the shared spoken parts of the mass. In short, too often, in too many parishes, a group of strangers gather together for private devotion. In addition, Searle and Leege point out, too much attention has been given to secondary environmental symbols like banners and not enough to helping people experience the power and meaning of the primary symbols used in worship: bread, wine, water, oil, and fire.

I do not attempt here to offer easy, facile approaches for the renewal of prayer and liturgy in our parishes. I am convinced that it is a special area that needs constant attention and effort.

CONCLUSION

A woman asked me recently at a meeting, "What are the signs that indicate a parish has indeed renewed itself around the eight constants?" My answer disappointed her. I told her that there was no graduation or arrival in terms of the issues of renewed vision, priorities, small groups, ministry, structures, calendar, tone, and prayer and worship. They all require ongoing effort, learning, failures, and progress. I do believe that they are and will be the issues that hold the key to ongoing parish renewal.

3

Inactive or Alienated Parishioners: New Dimensions for Ministry of Care

Jesus kept bad company. The Scriptures record that Jesus' style of ministry included a sensitivity to and compassion for some types of folks that many of the religious leaders thought were not the type of people to whom a true Messiah would minister. Jesus' concern was for the sinner, the sick, the socially rejected. If Jesus were to physically reappear today, I doubt whether He would focus His time and effort on some of the things in which organized religion invests time and effort.

Jesus probably would articulate the value of worship, while at the same time spending much of His time with those who have few ties to organized religion but who nonetheless have needs for meaning and healing. I think Jesus would especially want to reach out to those who once came to the parish but who now have little or no relationship with their church of origin.

One of the key demographic areas for evangelical focus and ministry is the inactive or alienated member. These are the people who for a variety of reasons have largely disassociated themselves from involvement with Church or parish. The inactive or alienated member is one of the significant target populations mentioned by Paul VI in his 1975 *Evangelii Nuntiandi,* as he attempted to articulate a kind of blueprint for evangelization for the Roman Catholic Church.

Though the terms *inactive* and *alienated* mean much the same thing in many instances, they admit of a shade of difference in the stories of some people. Some people become inactive (minimal or no worship or personal involvement in Church-related activities) without also personally experiencing some degree of anger, hurt, antipathy, or resentment toward Church or parish. Some people, on the other hand, are inactive *and alienated.* Alienated people are inactive quite often because of a subjectively perceived hurt or disappointment that they have experienced.

The following pages focus specifically on the evangelization of, or ministry to, the inactive or alienated member. The chapter is built upon the presumption that parishioners ought to be trained to engage in this ministry. I will offer some insights into the dynamics of religious alienation. I will also offer practical suggestions on how to reach out and minister to the inactive or alienated member, based on successful models from around the country. The chapter is divided into three levels in which parishioners can be trained.

LEVEL I OF TRAINING:
Understanding Why People Leave

The basic step in training for the ministry of reconciliation is helping trainees understand why people leave—the emotions behind their reasons for alienation as well as the reasons themselves. As the studies on this phenomenon mount, it becomes evident that there is no one reason for alienation from the Church. This section summarizes some of the more important findings on the inactive member.

Emotions Present in the Inactive Member

Research as well as informal experience with inactive or alienated members reveals rather commonly experienced emotions, often experienced in combinations or clusters with each other. I mention here the most frequently spoken of or shared.

1. Anger. Quite a few inactive members are angry with the Church, at God, or with specific representatives of the Church. The Church, as an institution, might have disappointed them personally. God may be looked on as the cause of a great loss or period of suffering. Priests, staff members, or fellow parishioners may have personally offended or disappointed them. Anger most frequently flows from violated expectations. This is true in all interpersonal relationships, and in church or parish life. Anger carries with it a network of other emotions, or shades of hostility: frustration, rage, cynicism, and isolation from the anger-producing source.

2. Hurt.   Often hurt is indistinguishable from anger, or they are flip sides of the same coin. People who feel hurt by the Church often go through some of the same stages of emotional erosion that a marital relationship goes through in the process of divorce. In divorce, which is essentially an emotional process before it ever becomes a legal process, two people pass through various stages of mutually perceived hurt.

- *Disillusionment.*   The mythic, overromanticized view of one's partner begins to melt, revealing the reality and humanity of the other person. One can begin to relate to that reality, or allow the relationship to slip into another stage.
- *Deterioration.*   Without serious therapeutic efforts on the part of both parties, the relationship, like any living organism, slips into gradually increasing stages of deterioration and disrepair.
- *Emotional disengagement.*   To avoid further pain, one or both parties begin to cut emotional ties with each other. Depending on the degree of intentionality and personal choice involved in the disengagement, this often can be the beginning of the death of the relationship. It is hard to repair a marriage after this stage.
- *Emotional divorce.*   The relationship, in effect, dies. Though sometimes, through heroic efforts on the part of both spouses and perhaps a therapist, or through the intervention of spiritual healing, the relationship may be resuscitated, most often this stage is the end of the relationship.
- *External activity that announces divorce.*   Through legal action, new romantic interests, geographical moves, and other behaviors, spouses announce to the world that their commitment to each other has ceased to exist.

Though obviously not a perfect parallel, I have seen the process of religious alienation assume configurations that are very similar to these stages of emotional divorce.

3. Apathy.   Many inactive or alienated people speak of a boredom or ennui concerning religious matters. This apathy can stem from a number of dynamics. Some spiritual apathy flows from the inactive member's own changing lifestyle. As some people get swept up in the busyness of work and relational responsibilities, organized religion becomes a back-burner issue, or no issue at all.

Some people report an apathy that is a consequence of a parish whose programs, preaching, or dominant spiritual tone does not touch "where they live," or help them live. Some apathy is symptomatic of buried feelings of hurt or resentment toward the faith community.

4. Longing.   Many who have minimized their contact with the Church speak of a deep longing present within them. The longing is for the comfort, familiarity, and shared meaning system of belonging to a church or parish. Despite the longing, other conflicting life issues block a pattern of return. Some research indicates that many inactives would at least consider returning if the invitation were extended.

5. Guilt.   This emotion also needs nuancing. The guilt of the alienated member sometimes takes the form of an uneasiness that comes from violating a previously sacred family or personal life pattern, that is, involvement in the Church. With other people, guilt is a blocking force that keeps one from returning to church. A person can be engaged in behavior that seems morally incongruent with church involvement. He or she is unwilling to let go of the behavior or moral pattern, yet feels it is nonetheless inappropriate for a church member. Thus, a guilt syndrome develops that is equivalent to a feeling of unworthiness.

Research on Drop-Out Patterns

Several studies stand out in recent years as significant statements about the alienation problem in the Church. As they are summarized, it will become evident that there is no one single reason that can be named as *the reason* people become alienated from active involvement. All of the following categories reflect the various realities of people's lives.

   To further clarify matters, let us retrieve the functional definition of the unchurched formulated by George Gallup, Jr., in the late 1970s. This definition was used by the American bishops as they began their increased efforts at evangelizing in the years after the publication of *Evangelii Nuntiandi* (Paul VI, 1975). This approach classifies the alienated or inactive Catholic as a subgroup of the broader category of the unchurched. For Gallup and the bishops, the unchurched were defined as any people who do not volitionally attend a worship service at least twice during the course of the year, besides special events like Christmas, Easter, weddings, and funerals. We proceed now to some of the more important studies.

1. In his book *Who Are the Unchurched?*[1] J. Russell Hale describes the unchurched from an existential viewpoint—who are they, and why are they staying away? He lists many types. I include here the ones that seem to be the most common within Catholic experience.

- *Anti-institutionalists.* These people still see *institution* as the primary metaphor with which the Church approaches people. As with most institutions, the Church appears to such people to be self-absorbed and self-perpetuating, rather than in service to people and the world.

- *Nomads.* America has become a mobile society. People involved in business commute each day between major cities in the same way suburbanites drive to the office downtown. Business also necessitates relocation for individuals and families, in some cases, every few years. In this nomadic lifestyle, many people fail to sink deep relational roots—in a neighborhood, an apartment or condo complex, or a parish. Many people do not even register in their parish upon arriving. Parochial schools and CCD programs around the country are talking about a new phenomenon that demands new forms of ministry, education, and religious socialization: the unevangelized, uncatechized, unsacramentalized child or adolescent. Such a young person, though culturally Catholic, has had no long-term relationship with a faith community. Programs of welcome for the new-comer, as well as a regular calling ministry, are needed to make contact with these people.

- *Pilgrims.* It would be inaccurate to think or speak of alienated Catholics in pejorative, unfair, judgmental terms. Many of the unchurched and alienated are deeply spiritual people who maintain an active prayer life and are quite personally committed to God and Christian values. Among the many unchurched and alienated are those that Hale refers to as pilgrims. Pilgrims are searching for life's meaning and also for a church or faith community in which to express their faith. Pilgrims are not finished yet. In their spiritual quest, they have not yet come upon a religion or spiritual family that they choose for themselves. Many pilgrims fall into the category of young adults who are in transition from "borrowed faith" to "owned faith."

- *The locked out.* Feeling hurt, left out, unwanted, or rejected is a result of reality being interpreted by a person's unique perception system. Sometimes the hurtful word or gesture has been there in reality; sometimes it has not. What is undeniable

[1] Washington, D.C.: Glenmary Research Center, 1978.

is that one *feels* hurt because of the way he or she sees things. Such is the case of the locked out—the many people who have had negative experiences with priests or other staff members. Included among the locked out are those who feel that they do not fit because their lifestyle is at variance with official Church teaching, i.e., divorce, birth control, abortion, homosexuality, and so on. In short, these people feel as if they have been locked out of active participation.

2. Andrew Greeley, in *Catholic Schools in a Declining Church,*[2] summarizes many feelings and thoughts about why people become inactive. He groups these into the following four models of explanation.

- *The "It Would Have Happened Anyway" model.*   This model of explanation says that inactive Catholics simply are reflections of the increasingly secularized culture around them. The high level of education and sophistication of most Catholics makes much of what the Church has to offer appear irrelevant.
- *The "Reaction against the Council" model.*   This model says that many people have simply been turned off by all the changes in the Church in the past fifteen to twenty years. Some have experienced the past years as innovation upon innovation. "The changes" have been poorly explained in many corners of Catholic life, and therefore they have been poorly understood. This understanding gap has led to a widespread alienation.
- *The "Meat on Friday" model.*   This model speaks of alienation and inactivity as symptoms of a dominolike disintegration of Catholicism. Adherents to this model see the allowing of meat on Friday and other similar liberalizing moves by the Church as little steps that led to the questioning of other heretofore sacred theories and practices: papal infallibility, the ban on artificial contraception, premarital intercourse, and holy day and Sunday obligations.
- *The "Birth Control Encyclical" model.*   This model debunks much of the three previous models. People who espouse this model of explanation say that Vatican II and the theological, liturgical, and pastoral changes it effected were long overdue, and therefore welcome. They see the 1968 encyclical *Humanae Vitae* as the real turning point in American Catholic life. The document has become a symbol for these people—a symbol of Catholic leadership and authority that is radically out of touch with and uncaring for the ordinary Catholic. The fact that Paul

[2]Fairway, Kansas: Andrews and McMeel, 1975.

VI reached his conclusions, disregarding the advice given to him by dedicated Catholic lay people who made up an international commission, further antagonizes this group. *Humanae Vitae* undermined the credibility of Church leadership. Many, angered by leadership's apparent insensitivity, or feeling locked out by the Church's sexual ethics, have left the Church. Greeley himself feels that the fourth model of explanation is the one that is most representative of reality.

3. Andrew Greeley, writing more recently with his sister, Dr. Mary Durkin, has done further analysis of the alienation syndrome in their book *Angry Catholic Women*.[3]

- *Reaction against sexism.* Greeley and Durkin feel there are a growing number of women who can no longer support a church that seems to participate in institutionalized sexism. From the nonordination of women, to the lack of position power of many women working in pastoral ministry, to the sexist language of the lectionary and sacramentary, to the barring of little girls from serving as acolytes at mass, Church leadership is invested in the maintenance of the status quo, a male-dominated Church. Sexism is leading many women to estrangement from their church of origin, the seeking of roles in other Christian churches, or the development of underground, Catholic base communities of women.

4. Dean Hoge, in *Converts, Dropouts, and Returnees*,[4] provides additional descriptions of the inactive or alienated.

- *Family tension dropouts.* As mentioned earlier, the existential reality of most adolescents and young adults is that they operate out of a kind of borrowed faith. They have yet to articulate and live out of their own "owned faith." The family tension dropout foregoes regular church involvement in the process of rebelling against or individuating from the world of his or her parents. The family tension dropout may continue in a chronic state of alienation, or experience alienation as a step in the pilgrimage toward owned faith.

- *Intermarriage dropouts.* The marriage of a Catholic to a nonpracticing Protestant, an unchurched person, or an active member of another religion can influence the religious practice of the Catholic. Typical patterns are becoming lukewarm in one's own faith practice, or gravitating toward the religious practice of one's spouse.

[3]Chicago: Thomas More Press, 1984.
[4]New York: Pilgrim Press, 1981.

- *Lifestyle dropouts.* Hoge honestly faces the reality that the alienation of some is of their own choosing. Some people simply develop values, attitudes, and behavior patterns that are at variance with the gospel or with regular church attendance and membership. The yuppie lifestyle, the bar scene, the job, success, and achievement receive the investment or attention one had given to faith or religious practice.

- *Antichange/not enough change dropouts.* Hoge presents a tension in which the Church is caught: two groups claiming alienation for diametrically opposed reasons. As already noted in analyzing Greeley's material, some complain that the Church has changed too much, too quickly. Others see the Church in a glacierlike fashion, changing too slowly. Both perceptions have contributed to this dropout syndrome.

- *Spiritual-need dropouts.* This is a particularly distressing phenomenon. Most of us know Catholics who now attend non-Catholic services or Bible study. Many of them fall into the category of spiritual-need dropouts. At a critical point in their faith development, the Catholic experience or the Catholic parish/institution did not speak to them, help them, minister to them. Many people who make up this subgroup speak of the poor quality of Catholic preaching, the neglect of Scripture in our culture and their simultaneous hunger for Scripture, or the anonymity that exists at Catholic masses and other gatherings. Spiritual-need dropouts either develop a spiritual privatism that does not sink root in any tradition, or they gravitate to another Christian tradition.

Some national leaders in evangelization speculate that young spiritual-need dropouts will be back within ten to fifteen years. My own experience of these dropouts is not as positive. Others say that many of them are being fed elsewhere, so why should we get overconcerned? I rejoice that many of them are fed elsewhere, but an unrelenting question for me is, Why can't we feed them? What do we need to learn—for example, from evangelical movements—to better minister to such people?

Hoge also offers some valuable insights into what brings people back to active church participation. Some of the areas that weaken participation can in turn lead people back. Significant among them is being married to someone for whom active church participation is a strong value. The strong witnessing of the active individual can encourage an inactive member. Hoge also found family life to be a motivating force in adults' return to participation. The religious education and socialization of children can create the milieu or environment for a revaluing of church membership. Just as there are spiritual-need dropouts, there are also spiritual-need returnees, that is, people for whom a hunger and thirst for meaning and spirituality eventually leads them back to worship and other involvement.

5. Finally, we will consider the insights of Dr. John Savage, some of which are contained in his book *The Apathetic and Bored Church Member.*[5] Savage has based his theories on years of experience and research. While not refuting any of the findings of the writers that we have already spoken of, Savage's concept of the alienation pattern or syndrome focuses on deeper levels of human experience. In other words, any of the reasons mentioned by Hale, Greeley, Durkin, or Hoge are probably symptomatic of a deeper malaise or difficulty.

Savage believes that the typical candidate for "dropping out" has within his or her lifestyle a cluster of anxiety-producing situations. He notes that the beginning of the drop-out pattern may have little to do with the Church. It has to do rather with life. A drop-out candidate might simultaneously be experiencing a pinch from the economy, the strain of mid-life marriage, and the confusion of parenting adolescents. In the midst of these anxiety-producing situations, many dropouts experience what Savage calls "the event." In "the event," the drop-out candidate, with different clusters of pain present in his or her life, interfaces with a congregation, staff member, or some representative of the community. It could be an encounter in the Religious Education Office, the vestibule of the church, or an office in the rectory. The essence of "the event" is that the drop-out candidate expects the parish to somehow be sensitive to his or her pain, to hear his or her cry for help which often is not clearly articulated. "The event" is characterized by the Church not hearing deeply enough, and apparently not caring enough. Often "the event" consists of a bureaucratic or legal response to deeply personal crises and issues.

Savage feels that there is a waiting period during which the drop-out candidate goes through a "faith spasm," not quite knowing what to do with God and the Church. But over the course of some weeks the faith spasm resolves itself. Most dropouts rediscover a personal spirituality, but they redirect their "church energy." The time and attention given to church involvement is redirected toward recreational activities, social services, or family issues.

[5] Pittsford, N.Y.: Lead Consultants, 1981.

Finally, Savage uses two metaphors to describe a person in the drop-out pattern. Some, he says, become "skunks." Extroverted in nature, they "spray" the environment with their anger, hurt, and pain. The focus of their spraying is the Church. Other, more introverted personality types become "turtles." They have a tendency to perceive themselves as unworthy of affiliation with the Church.

Implicit in Dr. Savage's analysis is an insight into how we can best minister to the alienated and inactive member. Rather than approaching these people with a strategy to "save" them, or a plan to manipulate a decision for Christ, parishes should approach the inactive member with an attitude of care. Care should be focused on the inactive member as a person—a hurting person. Some of those hurts are related to the Church; others are deeply rooted in the fabric of the person's personal life.

We do not get people back to church by trying to get them back to church. Rather, people may return to church if they meet and relate to Christian people who have genuine concern and compassion for their fellow person. It is not manipulative monologue but nonmanipulative dialogue that is an attractive, inviting experience for people.

A Ministry of Care and Reconciliation

For some time now we have trained and commissioned parishioners for the pastoral care and visitation of the sick. It is a ministry that many feel called to and in fact do well. Yet some of the same people involved in care of the sick would shy away from a similar care for the inactive member. In fact, across the country, training for and involvement in care for the inactive are not high priorities for staffs and congregations. What is the turnoff or difficulty? Perhaps ministry to the sick provides a ministerial setting that contains more "controls" for the minister, or that produces more situations where "the expected" will take place, than ministry to the inactive does. How will the inactive member receive the evangelist or caller? What will his or her stories, complaints, and difficulties be? Outreach to the inactive contains more unpredictable factors than the typical care of the sick does.

Perhaps also we think that we have to have all the answers for an alienated member's questions or problems with the Church. Or maybe we think the only success in such ministry is achieved when someone who has been away returns to the Church because of our time with them. The fact is, we need to approach alienated members with the same compassion, care, and desire to bring the Lord's healing into their heart as we do in caring for the physically broken. With the alienated member, so often what is needed is a listening ear, a kind word, and a prayerful spirit. We ought to take some of the fright out of this ministry by seeing it and packaging it as an extension of the parish's already existing "care" programs.

Somewhere in the Middle Ages, our concept of reconciliation became terribly narrow. We relegated it to the ritual of private confession to a priest and the reception of absolution. Even the addition of four new ritual formats in 1976 has not widened our Catholic perspective. The mandate the community has from Jesus is to become communities of healing and reconciliation. While sacramental confession and absolution can be part of that, it is by no means the exclusive means of reconciliation. The Church's and parishes' charge to reconcile admits of a variety of ministries, activities, and programs intended to heal brokenness and communicate forgiveness. Reaching out to inactive members, telling them there is a community that cares for them, issuing a welcome to them and helping them reenter the parish, should they so desire, is indeed existential, real reconciliation. It is reconciliation *being lived and experienced.* Are we in the midst of a reconciliation crisis as is sometimes lamented by the sacramental and liturgical experts? Perhaps the post-Vatican II Church has begun to find new ways to continue the Christian community's mandate to reconcile.

LEVEL II OF TRAINING:
Contracting for a Visit via the Phone

Some years ago, when I first started training parishioners for home visitation, I encouraged the practice of "cold calls." *Cold calls* was a term I used to describe the practice of simply going to the homes of the target population without any previous contact. While we had tremendous success with this style, I am surprised that we did. Calling on someone at his or her home without a preliminary contact of some kind is not respectful of the time of the person being called. In the last few years, consciousness has been raised by the media about the prevalence of violence and sexual abuse. These alarming stories make many people very reluctant to allow someone whom they do not know into their homes. So, in more recent years, I have included in training the importance of preliminary contact, at least through a phone call, with people who are to be visited.

Choosing a Target Population

A personal ideal of mine is to see the calling ministry as something other than a ministry focused only on inactive or alienated parishioners. If the calling ministry is seen against the broad background of the entire parish, then calling can become a way to (1) support and nurture active members and get in touch with their needs; (2) reach out in a stance of reconciliation toward the inactive; (3) establish ecumenical ties with people of differing denominations; and (4) welcome unchurched people who may be looking for a church family.

After being trained recently in Chicago, some five hundred callers returned to differing parishes. Each parish decided on a unique target group within the parish that they wanted to visit within a six-week period. Some parishes chose to call on parents of first communicants. Others chose to visit parents of children celebrating Reconciliation for the first time. Some parishes called on people whose names were put on cards at mass one Sunday and identified as people who were indeed inactive and would benefit from a visit. A tool such as the following could help with such an effort.

REQUEST FOR A HOME VISIT

Dear Staff and Evangelization Team,

I feel that it would be helpful if someone could visit this person during the days of the home visitation.

NAME _____

ADDRESS _____

_____

PHONE _____

Helpful comments in understanding the person's alienation from the Church:

_____

_____

_____

Please return this form to the parish, either at the Eucharist on weekends or at the rectory/parish center.

Other parishes, under a code of confidentiality, scrutinized financial records for the names of those who rarely use envelopes and therefore may be inactive. This strategy needs to be done with a great deal of care since some people who worship regularly may not use envelopes.

I could go on with examples of target groups. The point is this: In rotating target groups, a parish could have "material" for the calling ministry for years and years. I caution parishes to begin this ministry only if the parish is going to have a long-term commitment to it. Just as a parish would not arbitrarily cease a ministry to the sick or the grieving, neither should a calling ministry to hurting or inactive members and other types of people be seen as arbitrary or short term.

Four Touchstones for a Preliminary Phone Call

Once the target population has been chosen, each caller can decide how and when he or she can visit the number of people assigned to him or her from the target population. Approximately a week before a home visit is intended, the caller should telephone the person(s) to be visited. The phone call has a four-fold purpose.

1. To introduce the person to the calling ministry and the reason for it. I feel it is best to explain home visitation as an attempt on the part of the parish to get away from the parish plant and into the homes and lives of people. Home visitation is an existential, relational way of getting into the needs of people. It is a vehicle by which the nature of a local neighborhood can be seen more clearly, and the ministries of the parish shaped to address the needs. It should not be stated that home visitations are an attempt to get people back to church.

2. To establish the time of a call. Experience has shown me that callers need to arrange an appointment, a definite time, with someone whom they are seeking to visit.

3. To establish the length of the call. Before the visit, callers can give people a healthy sense of control over what is going to happen if there is agreement relative to the length of the visit. An optimum length is from fifty to sixty minutes. If a caller perceives that someone is reluctant to give that much time, go with the person's lead and accept the time he or she is willing to share.

4. To establish the place of the visit. While the most typical place for a calling experience is the home, some people, because of some domestic variable, might prefer to meet in a place other than the home. One such situation might involve someone who is living with an alcoholic, an addict, or an emotionally troubled person. Often, in such situations, it is hard to predict the mood that the problem person might be in when the day of the visit arrives, and thus a neutral meeting place would be safer than the home. Again, I advise trainees to go with such a person's lead—as long as the meeting place is a mutually agreed upon public place, like a restaurant or coffee shop.

The caller should leave his or her phone number with the person to be visited so that he or she can contact the caller if there is a need for rearranging the time, or if the person has decided against the possibility of the visit.

LEVEL III OF TRAINING:
Skills for Effective Relating on a Home Visit

While those Christians of a fundamentalist or evangelical orientation stress extensive training for their callers, most of the training is oriented toward "making the decision for Christ happen." Our strategy is certainly to hope for a decision for Christ, wherever and whenever that might come. But more basic concerns for training are to help callers feel comfortable with those on whom they call, and behave in such a way as to effect a sensitive, compassionate meeting with another individual.

The following are basic skills for effective human relating on a call. Other training models might include more sophisticated levels of human relations training. The presumption here is that the level of relational interaction in a home call will remain rather basic, and that those skills that might be characterized as "deeper" or "more sophisticated" are the concerns of those more intimately involved in the helping professions.

Attending and Body Language

Any of us who have had the experience of trying to sincerely communicate with another human being, only to have that person send us a mixed message by looking over our shoulders or beyond us to someone else, already know the importance of body language. What we do with our eyes, arms, legs, and body position is often more significant than the words we speak. Analysts of public speaking and drama report that only a small fraction of a communicator's input on an audience is his or her verbal input. More significant is the cumulative effect of body usage, tone of the personality, and the overall effect communicated. Below is a checklist for this particular segment of skills.

1. Eye contact.   Maintaining good eye contact is vital for good communication.

2. Posture.   Gently focusing one's body toward the person being visited nonverbally communicates care for that person.

3. A posture of openness.   We can use our limbs to communicate. Sometimes folded arms can be saying "I am afraid of you" or "I don't want to let you into my world—or enter yours!" Crossed legs can communicate similar messages. Whatever posture that we occasionally catch ourselves in, it is a good discipline to ask ourselves, "What might I be communicating nonverbally to people around me?"

4. Mirroring.   While the three items above might be called *attending* behaviors, callers need to be conscious also of *mirroring* behaviors. Mirroring might sound at first to be a contradiction of what has been discussed above. Mirroring balances out attending, or is in tension with attending. Mirroring refers to the attempt on the part of the caller to mirror back to the person being visited the emotional tone the caller feels is coming from the other person. Mirroring is also done through body language, verbal tone, and vocabulary. When someone mirrors another, he or she tries to portray in bodily tone some of the same feeling that is present in the other person. Mirroring tempers attending, so that we are always respecting the space and feelings of the person we are visiting. Mirroring necessitates a basic understanding of some of the insights of the school of communication known as neurolinguistics.

As mentioned in Chapter 2, neurolinguistics teaches that all of us have the capacity to experience reality on three different channels: auditory, visual, and kinesthetic. The auditory channel is the one through which we hear and listen to ideas. On the visual channel, we see (imagine) scenes, pictures, and images. On the kinesthetic level, we experience emotions; we feel. Neurolinguistic experts maintain that most of us shut down one or more of our channels. Part of mirroring involves watching for cues and clues for the channel through which a person takes in and interprets experiences and reality. Thus a caller must adjust his or her style of communication to fit the dominant channels of the person being visited. With an auditory-dominant person, a caller might adjust his or her vocabulary to include more ideas and hearing-oriented words. With a visual person, stories, picture words, and images are effective. With kinesthetic people, the caller might choose words that are more feeling and emotional in nature.

Through mirroring, a caller respects the space of the person being called on. Mirroring also helps callers enter more deeply into communion with those being visited.

A caller needs to decide which of the skills—attending or mirroring—is more effective in a given encounter.

Listening for Facts and Feelings

Much writing and training has been done in the area of active listening in recent years. From parents to teachers to corporate executives, listening has been an often overlooked skill that has been retrieved, revalued, and practiced in a variety of training sessions and seminars around the country. The work of Robert Carkhuff, Gerard Egan, and Thomas Gordon, among many others, has emphasized the importance of active listening.

In training others for active listening, I have found two words helpful in simplifying the activity. Those two words are *facts* and *feelings*. The goal of active listening is empathy, that is, *feeling with* a person, knowing what he or she feels. In training for active listening, a person needs to practice focusing on and naming another person's *feelings*. In addition to feelings, however, active listening involves a probing for the circumstances, the events, and the *facts* that prompted the feelings. Training, therefore, necessitates practicing a disciplined focusing on the *feelings* of a person relative to a given period in his or her life, and the *facts* (circumstances) that prompted those feelings.

I suggest that calling ministers, or anyone interested in growing in the skill of listening, keep a model sentence in mind as they try to actively listen to someone they are visiting. That model sentence is:

When _____ happened, you felt _____.

Not everyone's words fit the simplicity of that sentence. However, the sentence can be used as a kind of laser that cuts through a person's verbal content and gets to the heart of his or her communication. The model sentence, used as a mental discipline on the part of the listener, challenges the listener to focus on two simple realities as he or she listens: *What is this person feeling?* and *What happened that prompted these feelings?*

In the visitation of active or inactive members, calling ministers, using the "facts and feelings" model sentence, frequently hear comments like the examples that follow. (Note: Such comments frequently are not spoken as "clearly" as they appear here. Rather, the active listener, using the "facts and feelings" discipline, "organizes" input from the speaker.)

- "When the priest did not attend my mother's wake, I felt hurt."
- "When the only contact I had with that parish for a year was a request for money, I felt discouraged and disappointed."
- "When no one visited my son in the hospital, I felt bitter and angry."
- "When God allowed my husband to die such a cruel death at such a young age, I felt quite doubtful about what I previously believed about Him."

I reemphasize that "the data" are rarely communicated as clearly as these examples would indicate. Rather, these are examples of the disciplined listening, decoding, and translation of the active listener. Most of us communicate in "coded" or multilayered messages. The active listener attempts to decode a person's communication input to get the person's bottom-line facts and feelings.

The active listener, however, must "test reality" to see if his or her perceptions of another person's facts and feelings are accurate. The next skill that we turn to is a way of doing that.

Paraphrase and Reflection Back

How does a minister, a parent, a helper, or any active listener know whether he or she has indeed accurately heard and named another person's facts and feelings? The listener has to, in a way, ask, "Have I heard you accurately?" This section explores some simple ways to do that.

Recently, in trying to make sense of a person's communication to me about her past, I said something that I felt accurately summed up what she had said. I said that she seemed to have lived in a rather sheltered and idealized environment as she grew up. I immediately sensed a resistance on her part to what I had said, a defensiveness. On reflection, I can see the dysfunctional part of my communication. The style in which I communicated was judgmental. I transmitted a message to her that said "I know who you are and what you are about," rather than a message that said "I am struggling to try to understand you."

Calling ministers, all committed to active listening, need to remember the importance of *tentativeness*. Tentativeness is an attitude—a communicable attitude—that says, "I do not have you figured out, or fit into my own set of stereotypes. I have some hints of what I think you are saying and feeling, and I would like to try to see if I am accurate." The active listener ought to communicate a tentativeness, a wondering that seeks confirmation from the speaker.

An active listener can practice this tentative attitude in training and "on the scene" by using comments like "I'm wondering . . ." or "Could it be . . ." or "Help me with this . . ." Such tentative preliminary remarks can then be followed by the active listener's paraphrase of the facts and feelings that he or she has perceived in listening.

When I first began pastoral ministry, I used to dread hospital visits. The dread was from my own "private logic," a presumption that I ought to have a profound, meaningful insight into and verbal comment for each suffering person I came upon. I gradually began to see, as I grew in ministerial experience, that I did not have to have all the answers. I needed only to show that I understood how people were feeling. If I caught a person's facts and feelings, then most situations called next for a paraphrase and reflection back to the speaker of what I was hearing. This took the form of a tentative, implicit question: "This is what I heard; am I correct?"

Let us pause to look at what a tentative paraphrase and reflection back might look like, using examples of discerned facts and feelings already mentioned.

- "Let me check out whether I am hearing you correctly. No parish priest attended your mom's wake, and that hurt you. Am I hearing you correctly?"
- "Could it be, then, that you are disappointed with the parish because you feel it is too concerned with money?"
- "Is this accurate? No one from the parish visited your son while he was hospitalized, and this angered you?"
- "Is this what is going on inside of you? Your husband's premature death has caused you to doubt God's love and care?"

Reconciling Responses

People who become alienated from a church often develop stereotypic, generalized thinking about organized religion, or their parish in particular. These stereotypes become more deeply imbedded in consciousness as a long period of time passes. Lack of time, presence, and communication between an alienated member and the community worsens the stereotypic thinking. A parishioner who is willing to be part of outreach to inactive or alienated members can be taken off guard, or experience a kind of "communications shipwreck," if he or she is not aware of, and somewhat prepared to respond to, generalizations or stereotypes.

Practicing *reconciling responses* with a team of callers involves going through some of the more typical generalizations, offering some model responses to such generalizations, and facilitating the group toward the generation of additional, group-created responses. Reconciling responses are not an attempt to provide an easy, facile response to a long-festering hurt or wound. Rather, it is an acceptance of the reality of the hurtful situation, while gently nudging the conversation in a positive, healing direction. It must be used with the other skills listed here, especially active listening. If used by itself, divorced from other facilitating skills, it could further alienate someone by minimizing or not attending to his or her hurt. Below are listed some model generalizations or comments that might serve as a starting point for trainees to rehearse reconciling responses.

MODEL IDEAS FOR DEVELOPING RECONCILING RESPONSES

Generalization	Ideas on Which to Build a Response
"I have been divorced (and remarried), and I know I have no place in the Church."	• Inform the person of the Church's efforts to minister to the divorced. • Inform him or her of the new possibilities for grounds for annulment and second marriages. • Be aware of divorce support groups in the area.
"The Catholic Church does not value the Bible."	• Own the criticism; for years we have not put enough emphasis on God's Word. • Mention the centrality of both Old and New Testaments, as well as the homily, at each Eucharist. • Be aware of Scripture study groups in the area.
"The changes in the mass, some years ago, turned me off."	• Identify with the situation: either you or others you know have had difficulties accepting liturgical changes. • Mention the variety of liturgical styles present in the parishes in the area: traditional, choir, guitar, etc.

"The Church changed too much, too quickly. I was comfortable with the old Church."

- Again, identify with the situation, perhaps mentioning changes that you or others were uncomfortable with.
- Stress that the changes were not an alteration of revelation or doctrine but rather a shaping of style as to how things are done in the Church.

"The Church is too bureaucratic and institutionalized. It is quite different from the Church that Christ began."

- Admit that the "institution" is indeed one of the sides of the Church.
- State the ideal: The value of the institution is in helping the other sides of the Church shine forth, namely, the dimension of community.
- Own the problem that some have stressed the institutional dimension too much, too often.

"The Church is too slow in changing things like mandatory celibacy for priests and discrimination against women in leadership."

- Again, own the negativity: Like other institutions, the Church changes very slowly.
- Mention that the issues of celibacy and the role of women are seriously being studied on many levels of church membership.

"A priest or parish representative hurt or disappointed me."

- Apologize on behalf of the church family.
- Identify with the situation, sharing an example of how you have been hurt.
- Share the insight that *the people* are the Church, and therefore the Church is much bigger than one person who is offensive or who had a bad day.

"I no longer see a great need for organized religion in my life."

- Respect the person's feelings.
- Humbly share the difference that God and Church make in your life.

"To be honest, I have just gotten too busy (or lazy) and the Church has not been a high priority."

- Again, identify with the situation, talking about the busyness of your own life.
- Talk about the struggle in each person's life to prioritize well.

"I have trouble with the Church's sexual ethics. I disagree with the official teaching on birth control."

- Offer support, reminding the person of how many people are confused about sexual ethics and by different opinions about sexual matters present in the Church.
- Reassure him or her that many people are forming their own personal consciences, using the guidance of the Church.
- Mention that the post-Vatican II emphasis on personal moral responsibility has resulted in a plurality of opinions and behaviors.

"I wouldn't fit in the Church. My lifestyle has involved a lot that the Church doesn't agree with."

- Remind the person of the lifestyle of Jesus, always inclusive of all types of people.
- Talk about the truly Catholic nature of the Church—universal and inclusive.
- Speak of the Church as a church of sinners; we approach Church and Christ, not because we are already perfect, but because we need Him and each other in our imperfection.

Listening for Rules and Roles

Alfred Adler, like Carl Jung, eventually broke with his mentor, Sigmund Freud, because of growing disagreements over the nature of personality. While Freud saw the human personality as pushed and pulled by instincts and drives, Adler felt that beginning in childhood, human beings put together a vision of self, others, and life called the lifestyle. An important phrase in Adlerian psychology is *on purpose*. Adlerians feel most behaviors, thoughts, and feelings are on purpose, that is, intimately connected with and flowing from the personally constructed and chosen lifestyle. Though much of the dynamics of the lifestyle might function unconsciously, the style of a person's life flows purposefully from what he or she believes, or senses as important. The perception of what is important in life is shaped by how a person feels he or she can gain feelings of significance and importance from others and the world around him or her.

In short, Adlerians are always interested in what makes a person tick, what is important to or motivates him or her. Most of us play *roles* in life, and operate out of certain unwritten *rules*—all in pursuit of significance, importance, and belonging. Often we can only guess at the rules and roles of others to whom we are relating. This is especially true when our encounters with others are rather brief in nature.

This is often the situation with home visitation ministry. If we have only a few meetings with another person, we probably will not get to know that person well. Nonetheless, making hunches about what makes another person tick, or about the roles a person is playing in life and the inner rules that guide his or her life, can help the caller grow in understanding of the person visited. Listening for life rules and roles can also aid in discerning why one might have grown alienated from the Church.

In practicing this skill, trainees need to be cautioned about jumping to conclusions about another person's inner life. They also ought to be encouraged to see "rules and roles listening" as part of a bigger process of discernment and understanding of another person. Emphasis needs to be placed on the reality of process, or "coming to understand" the person visited.

Listening to What People Don't Say

Some time ago a woman spoke to me in my office about her son, who had an apparent drug problem. In the course of the conversation, she spoke of her son, herself, the drugs, the other children in the family and how her son related to them. She did not, however, mention her husband at all during the conversation. As she spoke, I found myself wondering more about what she did not talk about (namely, her husband) than about what she had mentioned. Gradually—and, I hope, sensitively—I moved toward inquiring about her husband. He was very much alive, living in the home. The woman also gradually revealed that she and her husband were at odds with each other about how best to handle their son. Hiding under the son problem was another one: marital conflict and discord.

By listening for something that she seemed to avoid, I was able to lead her into a conversation about a very problematic issue in her life.

Along with listening for rules and roles, listening to what people do not say is simply an internal discipline that may help a caller understand the person visited a little better. This skill—as well as caution, sensitivity, tentativeness in questioning, and a view toward "coming to know" a person—needs to be kept in mind. In all cases, if a person seems unwilling to talk about a given area, then that wish should be respected by the caller. A question about something obvious that is not being talked about should be presented only as the caller senses rapport is building up. The style of questioning should be gentle, so as to not harm that rapport.

Preparing Callers to Talk about Their Faith

Callers who are trained in evangelization skills in a fundamentalist, evangelical program like *Evangelism Explosion* have up-front goals in training and in visiting homes. These goals include the caller's sharing of his or her own faith story, followed by the invitation to the person who is called upon to "be saved," or to accept Jesus Christ as Lord and Savior. While many of these evangelical movements seem to be having numerical success in winning people to Christ, I feel there are also dysfunctional dimensions to their strategies.

Leadership magazine (an ecumenical journal) recently studied hundreds of people across the country who had been visited by callers or evangelists. Most of the people called upon appreciated having been visited. But among those who did not appreciate the visits were those who felt manipulated by the callers. These people felt that the caller entered their home and "talked at them" about Jesus. Then, it seemed they were trying to push the person being visited toward verbalizing a decision for Christ. These evangelical strategies have little regard for listening to people's needs or trying to minister to people as they are, gradually guiding them along in a process of spiritual nurturance. In addition, the strategies seem to be rather presumptuous in that they suggest that God was not an important part of a person's life until the caller entered the home. In his book *Turning to Christ,* the late Episcopal priest Urban Holmes critiqued these evangelical approaches as a kind of hostile evangelization, which is often experienced by the person called upon as a kind of "emotional rape."

Home visitation without a grounding in faith, however, can become little more than what community organizations bring to a neighborhood: canvassing the area for the discernment of community needs. In the training programs that I have coordinated around the country for this ministry, I have strongly emphasized the importance of training people for sharing their faith. The nuance that I add, however, is that *faith stories should be shared only when it seems appropriate to the flow of the visit, aids the visit, and might be truly helpful for the well-being of the person visited.* Without practicing this discipline, the caller runs the risk of his or her faith story being perceived as a "one-upmanship" technique or, in some cases, a weapon to over-power the person being visited. We ought not to hit people over the head with the Bible or Jesus.

I also emphasize a sense of *congruency* in telling one's faith story. Too often faith sharing can become a "Can you top this?" exchange of heartache and misery, or the relating of peak spiritual moments. Because many people have not had such profound conversion experiences, they become reluctant to share the details of their own faith journey, feeling that their experiences are not as good as those of others. *Congruency* means that a caller's words ought to express accurately the changes that faith has brought into his or her life. In some cases, the words of a person's story might be quite passionate and dramatic. For many of us, the stories will be of simple, quiet, processlike shifts that have taken place in us over the course of time.

I usually give people in training an opportunity in the first few sessions to briefly write their own faith stories. The writing need only be notes that help the person remember significant moments in his or her pilgrimage. Then, after significant quiet time, trainees share as much as they are comfortable sharing in small groups. I have found that this technique rather quickly moves the group toward a feeling of bondedness and community, anchors calling training in a conversion spirit, and helps those in training to get a feel at the very outset of what evangelization is most about. The technique of writing and sharing stories also facilitates reflection on and discussion about some things that we too often take for granted: the difference that faith and Church have brought into our lives. Having written and shared their stories in training, callers have this resource ready and available in their memory and consciousness.

Information Gathering and Networking Skills

Home visitation ministers are in a position to do ongoing, fresh research into the needs and mood of a parish. Much of what they learn, however, can be lost or dismissed if it is not in some way recorded. Information gathering can be approached in two dif-ferent ways: *generally,* in terms of getting the pulse of the parish, and *personally,* that is, recording information about individuals in the parish. Briefly we will look at each approach.

Home visitation ministers can become valuable resources in regard to the parish as a community. As trends, needs, and opinions are generically shared by the callers among themselves and with the staff, parish leaders can begin to discern directions for future programs and ministries in the parish.

Information gathering can be approached also on an individual basis. Such individual record keeping is important from three vantage points. First, record keeping helps the caller remember important facts about the people he or she has visited, thus facilitating follow-up and ongoing visits. Second, accurate information about a person who has been called can help the caller do networking between the person called and the parish or neighborhood resources that the person may need. Third, ongoing record keeping can be used to update parish census information.

As I train callers, I encourage them to keep a note pad in the car, or elsewhere, so that after a visit they might jot down pertinent, important information. Some parishes have used an information form like the one on page 88. Information that is important to record includes the age of the person called, the number and ages of people in the home, special needs that are apparent in the home, and the apparent degree of the person's involvement in or alienation from the Church.

Anyone doing home visitation should possess two resources: information on services that are offered by the parish, and information about services offered by the town, village, or neighborhood. It is helpful to leave such information in the homes of those visited. The caller can also become a conduit, liaison, or networking person, connecting the visited person with a minister or agency that can help with a particular need.

When it comes to networking, bridging, or passing on any information, it is important for callers to respect and practice confidentiality. No important information should be networked or shared without the permission of the person called. Our enthusiasm to be helpful should not outweigh another person's right to privacy.

Need Discernment Skills

I often repeat this principle as I conduct training programs for outreach to the inactive: *You do not get people back to church by trying to get them back to church.* People may return to church if they meet a church member who genuinely is concerned about and cares for them. Stated another way, the goal of home visitation is not necessarily getting someone to return to church. In fact, a person may have more pressing needs than a return to

PARISH INFORMATION

Name of person visited _____

Address _____

Town _____ Zip _____

Phone _____ Name of spouse _____

Names of children _____ Age _____

_____ Age _____

_____ Age _____

_____ Age _____

_____ married _____ single _____ divorced

If Catholic: _____ active _____ inactive

Non-Catholic: _____

_____ unchurched _____ interested

Needs perceived or suggestions for the parish:

_____

_____

If inactive, reasons given:

_____

_____

Should this person be contacted by someone else? _____

Priest for pastoral care _____

Coordinator for religious education of children
or adult renewal or inquiry _____

Further comments of the lay evangelist _____

_____

_____

_____

_____

NOTE: The above is a model information card or sheet that can be filled out by the lay evangelist subsequent to the visit. The card should then be given to the pastor or evangelization director. In turn, the card can be given to the parish secretary or the designated committee secretary. Cards can be kept at the parish center as a data bank on parishioners and the neighborhood. Cards containing information that would benefit other parishes or denominations should be sent to the appropriate places. Cards indicating pastoral needs should be followed up on immediately.

regular church attendance. As a caller hears the stories of those whom he or she is visiting, it is important for the caller to focus on the question of what would be most helpful for this person right now in his or her life journey. Typical needs that can be overlooked if a caller is too focused on church attendance include sacramental care for a shut-in (in Catholic culture), support during or after a divorce, single parenting support, food pantry assistance, emotional or financial aid, and counseling or psychotherapy. While the caller is usually not the "delivery person" for such services, he or she can serve as a helpful conduit or facilitator, as stated earlier.

Invitation and Facilitating Skills

Much of this section is a reechoing of the two preceding sections. As information is gathered and needs are discerned, the caller can become, to the degree confidentiality permits it, an important "connecting person."

1. Invitation. If a caller senses a curiosity about the Church, it is helpful to have something offered locally that can tend to that curiosity. One such effort that has met with success in Chicago is a strategy called Catholicism Revisited. Catholicism Revisited is a catechumenate-like process that, while briefer than a true RCIA process, offers to a person a process of inquiry, growth, prayer, and community. Father John Forliti, a pioneer in a Minneapolis–St. Paul-based project called Alienated Catholics Anonymous, says that alienated members have some standardized, basic needs: new information about the Church, the opportunity to talk about and ventilate their feelings, and some positive experiences with churchgoing people.

Catholicism Revisited follows an RCIA-like rhythm of a general inquiry experience, followed by a number of catechetical experiences, followed by an opportunity for spiritual renewal and reconciliation with the Church. The last step, usually best experienced through a quality Lenten program, can flow into a Holy Week–Easter celebration of reconciliation. Finally, just as new members who have been initiated through the catechumenate are in need of a mystagogia or post-Easter process of learning and support, so also returnees are in need of ongoing, follow-up ministries. Two pieces of this process are analyzed in more detail in the following sections.

2. Homecoming. I have frequently employed a "Homecoming" evening as a beginning strategy for returnees. Calling ministers, should they be visiting around the time of a Homecoming, can extend a special invitation to alienated or inactive members to attend such an evening.

The outline for a Homecoming evening is simple. The key portion of the evening is "questions and answers." During this period, the staff and trained parishioners allow the alienated to voice their hurts and questions; then the leaders make an attempt to respond to them.

A Homecoming should be scheduled after some weeks of home visitation, advertising in the local press, talking about it at church, and asking the congregation to "pass the word" on to relatives and friends who have been alienated. The following is a model display ad that was placed in a local newspaper, announcing an upcoming Homecoming.

Inactive Catholics

Come and voice your feelings.
Come and learn about current Catholic thought.
You're invited home!

HOMECOMING

A night of discussion for inactive Catholics
SATURDAY, Nov. 17, 7:00 P.M.

ST. HUBERT CHURCH
729 Grand Canyon Pkwy.
HOFFMAN ESTATES
(in Clubroom of Church)

COME! BRING FRIENDS! NO OBLIGATION!
Call 588-7700

At an actual Homecoming, a staff member serves as a moderator or host. Scattered throughout the room are trained parishioners, some of them formerly inactive Catholics who have returned to active membership. With the host staff member is the rest of the pastoral staff. Both they and the trained parishioners know they can "break in" and offer input as the night progresses. The outline for a Homecoming is as follows:

   I. **Opening prayer and sharing of Scripture**
  II. **An initial input.**   The host explains the purpose of the evening and the flow of the evening's schedule.

III. Questions and answers. (Paper and pencils should be provided.) All attending are asked to make an anonymous list of issues, questions, or blocks that they have relative to contemporary American Catholicism. This part makes up the bulk of the meeting (about two hours), with each of the staff members commenting on issues raised by those attending. The host reads and facilitates the questions, taking care to avoid repeating questions that have already been answered. He or she should try to make this section dialogical and open in the sense of as many people as possible being invited to respond to the questions or issues.

IV. Summary. The host attempts to summarize the feelings and ideas shared during the session.

V. Invitation. The host extends an invitation to participants to engage in the Catholicism Revisited follow-up series. This follow-up consists of a catechetical update for returnees and their families.

VI. Closing prayer

VII. Fellowship. Time should be provided for a break during the two-and-one-half-hour session, as well as for refreshments and hospitality.

3. Catholicism Revisited. Returnees need time, catharsis, ventilation, healing, updating, spiritual renewal, and new, positive experiences of Church. One model of follow-up to a Homecoming evening is Catholicism Revisited. As indicated earlier, Catholicism Revisited is an attempt to capture for returnees some of the experiences of the catechumenate. The catechumenate, or Rite of Christian Initiation of Adults (RCIA), is a step-by-step process, in group or community, of joining the Church. While the process, discussed at length in Chapter 5 of this book, is designed for unchurched or non-Catholic people as a vehicle of conversion and inquiry into the faith tradition, it contains within itself values and behaviors that are paradigmatic for other ministries, e.g., ministry to the inactive member who may be returning.

The basic flow of the RCIA is presented on page 92 with both technical and rather popular terminology.

In the Homecoming–Catholicism Revisited model, Homecoming evening and home visitations serve as *stage 1*. Catholicism Revisited can function as *stage 2*, or a time for renewed understanding. The total community's Lenten program and Lenten liturgies are a natural way to experience *stage 3*. Easter, either in a public ceremony with the catechumens or a quiet moment in the context of Easter Eucharist, can constitute *stage 4*. *Stage 5* consists

Stage	Technical Terminology	Popular Terminology
1	Evangelization	Spiritual awakening
2	Catechumenate (catechesis)	Understanding faith
3	Purification	A time for discipleship and renewed holiness
4	Easter and Sacraments of Initiation	A time to revow to Jesus and Church
5	Mystagogia	Deepening faith, finding one's place in the community, possibly beginning to serve or minister

of follow-up ministries, trying to help the returnee find his or her new place in the community.

Catholicism Revisited can extend from five to ten sessions, depending on the nature of the group. To avoid a classroom or "schooling" motif, the following outline might be helpful for each session.

  I. Individual participant's journal writing of personal thoughts and feelings about the topic of that evening.

 II. Small group sharing of those parts of the journal entries that people are comfortable sharing.

 III. Personal witness talk on the topic of the session, ideally given by a lay person or parishioner (e.g., member of the evangelization team).

 IV. Theological update on the topic, either by a staff member or a trained parishioner.

  V. A return to the journal, to document any changes, shifts, new ideas, conclusions, affirmations, or areas of agreement that have resulted from the witness talk and/or update.

 VI. Discussion of the above journal entries, in small groups.

VII. Closing prayer, with ritual action focusing on the theme of the session.

Examples of possible update topics and appropriate rituals are:

- *"The Difference God Can Make"*—prayer with open hands, opening oneself to the Father's unconditional love
- *"Jesus: Teacher, Savior, and Lord"*—individual veneration of the cross
- *"A Church for the Kingdom"*—handshake of peace; Lord's Prayer with joined hands

- *"Sacraments as Vows"*—writing of personal vow or covenant with the Lord
- *"Morality as Responsibility"*—personal, quiet prayer of sorrow for sin; imposition of hands by leader minister
- *"Developing a Spiritual Program"*—quiet reflection, then individual sharing of one or two pieces of the participants' proposed daily spiritual programs
- *"Our Basic Book: The Bible"*—individual veneration of the Scriptures

Provision ought to be made for the formation and updating of the children of adult returnees. Their sessions could be held in another room but at the same time as the parents' sessions. Each session could close with families participating in the closing ritual.

Some parishes have chosen to use callers as part of other programs besides Homecoming and Catholicism Revisited. Some, for example, are adding callers and home visitation as a key piece in sacramental preparation (Baptism, Matrimony, Eucharist, Reconciliation, Confirmation). Home visitation penetrates the typical anonymity of such efforts and adds a real tone of sponsorship or accompaniment.

Handling Objections, Questions, Anger

People in training for the calling ministry need some practice in responding to the unpredictable. Callers are sometimes the recipients of objections to the Church or parish practices, questions about policies or theology, and anger about actual situations or generalizations that lurk in the perceptions of some of the people called upon. Let us briefly consider such situations.

Because this ministry inevitably involves objections to and questions about Church practice and theology, it is extremely important that the people chosen and trained for this ministry be current in their reading and understanding. Callers need not be theologians, but they should be well informed. However, even the best informed at times have questions put to them for which they have no ready answers. Callers need to be encouraged in training to not be afraid to say, in the midst of a visit, "I don't know; let me check on that for you." It is humble, in a healthy sense, to admit one's uncertainty about an issue and then seek out input or resources that can help both the caller and the called upon to learn and grow.

A principle for callers to keep in mind relative to objections and anger is that when someone articulates an objection or expresses anger, most often in the form of a generalization, the caller really needs only to own *the truth* of the statement. As a caller, I can apologize for a hurt a person feels or agree with some other truth in the objection or anger of a person, but I need not agree with the whole generalization or stereotype, which indeed might be filled with distortion or exaggeration. To please the person called upon, we need not agree with untruth.

Time Lining a Visit

I strongly suggest that callers try to imagine and stylize home visitation according to three movements: rapport building, dialogue, and closure. Perhaps stating those three movements seems like emphasizing the obvious. I have found, however, that without a sensitivity to the three movements, a caller can spend lots of time in rapport-building chitchat and never get to a meaningful dialogue, or can try to jump into a meaningful dialogue without first building rapport. Others build rapport, enter into dialogue, but do not bring the visit to fitting closure; and therefore they stay beyond their welcome, or leave with a feeling of unfinished business. In training, callers ought to critique each other concerning these three movements and how easily transitions were made to each one.

Supporting Fellow Callers: Debriefing

People in outreach to inactive members have a high burnout rate. In some parishes where this ministry has begun, people pass in and out of the ministry as if in a revolving door. Part of this burnout/revolving-door syndrome is due to a lack of discipline regarding regular meetings of callers. Callers and their trainers and supervisors need to meet at least monthly. At these meetings, callers can be helped to maintain the skills talked about in this chapter. Such meetings can also be a source of support for these ministers who often are "out there by themselves" doing this ministry. Ongoing skills training and mutual support are best provided for by callers sharing some of the stories they have actually experienced in the field, and role playing such stories with each other. Through peer interaction, much can be learned about alternate styles of approaching individual situations.

One way of insuring that support meetings happen is to schedule the meeting on a common day after a common period of calling. For example, callers gather at a central place, go out on visits, and after an agreed period of time, return and talk to each other about what happened in the field.

Callers should make a commitment for at least one year, and should expect to make at least two or three calls a month.

Follow-up

Both calls and processes like Homecoming–Catholicism Revisited need follow-up. Some evangelical Christians refer to this as "closing the evangelical back door." If the "back door" is not closed, people have a tendency to enter the Church by the "front door" and rather quickly exit through the "back door." Follow-up can be looked at from three perspectives.

1. A sponsoring relationship.   Someone who is called upon or experiences a returnee process has much the same needs as a catechumen. Among the most significant ministers for a catechumen are the sponsors and godparents. These are the Christian friends who support, accompany, and worship with the catechumens both before and after their process of inquiry. Inactives and returnees have much the same need for such support. Home visits, of a supportive nature, ought to follow the initial visit. A caller should be responsible for only seven to ten calls within a given time frame. The caller ought to "bond" with the person through several home visits, phone calls, invitations to functions, and so on, for up to a year. If the initial caller is unable to fulfill this sponsoring function, someone else should fill this role. (Note: The goal of outreach is a healthy relationship between the person visited and the evangelist. It is not the main goal of home visits to manipulate people to programs.)

2. Parish programs.   Outreach to the inactive member necessitates a number of programmatic responses. Some of the programs might already be in existence; some may need to be started. Significant categories of such programming include:

- Bible study
- Adult education, based on needs
- Divorce groups
- Widow/widower groups
- Missions and revivals
- Retreats
- Single parent groups
- Annulment information
- Young adult ministries

3. Ongoing parish renewal.   Strategies for parish renewal are discussed at length in Chapter 2. Suffice it to say here that inactives-returnees most probably will not return to a community that is not in the process of renewing itself in order to better share the gospel and minister to people's needs. Outreach to the inactive cannot be begun in a vacuum, but is a piece fitted into a larger picture of parish evangelization.

Other Strategies

Some parishes are not equipped, ready, or willing to begin the calling ministry, Homecoming, or Catholicism Revisited. For such communities, I include the following list of "other strategies" which express a concern for and willingness to reach out to inactive members.

1. Parish tone. Celebrants and parishioners need to work on developing a welcoming, hospitable attitude at worship and parish activities.

2. Total neighborhood canvas. After an ecumenical approach to training, Protestant and Catholic evangelists can visit all the homes in any area, informing them of the various Christian churches.

3. Telephone ministry. Some parishes choose to do most of their outreach via the telephone.

4. Parish registration and newcomers' program. By holding new-comers' breakfasts, making registration more of an experience of commitment, and other welcoming activities, parishes can evangelize people *before* they become inactive. Some Protestant communities use a "shepherding" process in which newcomers are attended to for their first few months in the community.

5. Ministries to significant or crisis moments. Weddings, wakes, funerals, funeral luncheons held in the parish hall, follow-up during the months of grieving, hospital and shut-in visitation are all excellent means of touching the inactive.

6. Healing activities. Developing a pastoral counseling program and opening the door to self-help groups (Alcoholics Anonymous, Alanon, Alateen, Families Anonymous, Narcotics Anonymous, Tough Love) have helped some parishes become known as centers for healing the active, inactive, and unchurched.

7. Parish newsletters. Since the inactive rarely receive a parish bulletin, a quarterly newsletter can inform them of activities.

8. Each one–reach one. At various times during the year, each active parishioner should be encouraged to reach out to at least one inactive or unchurched person and invite that person to something at the parish.

9. The family. Include parents in family-style sacramental preparation and in each year's curriculum for CCD and parochial school.

4

Evangelizing Youth

In a recent article of *Seventeen* magazine, a periodical targeted for adolescent females, author Joe Bell surveyed the religious attitudes of a representative study group of American teenagers. He was in pursuit of an answer to the question, Is there evidence of a renewal of religious, spiritual attitudes among teenagers in this country? His findings in this national study were surprising. Compared to teenagers in the sixties and seventies, teenagers of recent years seem more genuinely interested in and open to religion. However, this renewal of religious fervor is not being experienced in any sort of organized way in the mainline churches of the United States. Rather, young people are gravitating toward nondenominational Christian churches. In fact, a significant crossover has begun from the mainline churches (Catholic, Lutheran, Episcopal, and so on) to these nondenominational, youth-oriented churches.

As Bell searched for the reasons for the success of these churches or youth movements, several facts surfaced repeatedly: the music of traditional churches is old-fashioned, while the nondenominational churches use Christian rock; the young people's churches of origin have poor preaching, whereas the youth ministers of the newer churches speak to teens' real life problems and needs; while the young people may have been in religious education for years in their traditional churches, the newer youth churches first introduced them to Jesus and the Bible.

STRATEGIES FOR YOUTH EVANGELIZATION

I have been in youth work for over fifteen years. Someone who has greatly influenced my approach to youth is Erik Erikson. This developmental psychologist wrote many years ago that adolescence is not just a time for putting together one's sexuality and identity. In addition to undertaking those tasks, the adolescent also must begin the process of ideological commitment or values clarification. The failure to engage in this beginning of piecing together a values system results in values confusion, an adulthood oriented toward self-gratification but devoid of deeper meaning or a sense of responsibility to other people. Other researchers like Lawrence Kohlberg and James Fowler have supported Erikson's insight that the adolescent years are years that hold the possibility for beginning the search for one's own values system, and one's own "owned faith," to replace the borrowed faith that children receive from parents and religious educators. If Erikson, Kohlberg, and Fowler are correct, could one of the problems of mainline churches, in the area of youth evangelization, be that we are systematically "underwhelming" American youth? Just as young people reach the point of being able to give their hearts to spiritual values, perhaps we are not creatively present in their lives as Church, facilitating growth and conversion. At least for some young people, could the obvious conversion orientation of evangelical youth churches be the reason that they are crossing over and leaving their church of origin?

In Chapter 2, I briefly touched on youth ministry. I presented one of the primary strategies of evangelical youth movements, namely, the *organic growth* method. In quick summary, organic growth youth ministry refers to the process of a youth minister reduplicating himself or herself through the gradual development of a network of peer-to-peer youth ministers, each with the felt responsibility of welcoming new members. In this chapter, we will examine another of their strategies, *full-cycle youth evangelization.* Later in the chapter, we will explore the implications in this model for our own youth evangelization.

If there is a major flaw in Catholic youth ministry efforts, I think it is that we are spotty or sporadic in our efforts. One parish may have a socially oriented teen club; another might have a religious education program; still another might have a retreat program. But very few parishes across the country offer all such efforts, organized in a meaningful, logical way toward Christian growth and commitment. But this is the genius of evangelical efforts. Full-cycle youth evangelization is precisely the offering of many youth activities that are not offered at whim but are organized, in a process sort of way, toward conversion. One way that full-cycle youth evangelization could be visualized is shown in the diagram on page 100.

Notice the energizing pieces of this model: peer-to-peer ministry; a conviction that adolescents and young adults can, to some degree, experience conversion; a variety of youth activities organized in a process sort of way toward commitment; and the importance of verbalizing and ritualizing faith growth for young people. I believe that Catholic youth ministry, and the youth ministry efforts of other mainline churches, can create similar models of full-cycle youth evangelization. We have all the right pieces; we just need to learn how to lay them out in a meaningful process that facilitates growth. We can be—we ought to be—involved with young people in what Erikson called the crisis of ideological commitment vs. values confusion.

Adolescents have a natural need to affiliate, or to relationally bond. Our challenge is to offer them that "other place" where affiliation can take place in the context of healthy relationships and faith. Child psychologist Bruno Bettelheim, in a recent article in *US News and World Report,* said that children and teenagers listen to the loudest voice when it comes to values formation. He was implying that in some cases, churches, schools, and families are failing to do their job in values clarification. Thus, teenagers listen to the "loud voices" of movies, TV, rock music, and rock videos—voices that often portray acts of violence, sadomasochism, and explicit sex.

Though an ordained minister, I do not consider myself a prude. But I share in the sentiments of a concerned mother, in her late thirties, who recently wrote a guest editorial in *Newsweek* magazine. She confessed to being a lover of rock, but also to being concerned about the quality of rock music to which her children were being exposed. She closed her article by referring to an insight from Aristotle: music forms the imagination. I believe that the mother's concern is well founded, considering the statistics presented in Robert Coles and Geoffrey Stokes's recent study *Sex and the American Teenager.* In a national survey of the sexual mores and behaviors of American teenagers, the two researchers found that 53 percent of the females in their sampling and 46 percent of the males had experienced sexual intercourse by the age of eighteen. This 1985 study by Coles and Stokes was preceded by a similar study made in 1979 by Aaron Hass, in his book *Teenage Sexuality.* Hass also reported a high incidence of teenage sexual

MODEL FOR FULL-CYCLE YOUTH EVANGELIZATION

The Stage of Fun Seeker	The Stage of Becoming Spiritually Sensitive		The Stage of Becoming Christian	The Stage of Discipleship	The Stage of Becoming a Worker for Christ
The previously de-scribed peer-to-peer, organic growth model brings a young person into the social activities of the youth movement. This new member is immediately made a member of a small group or team under the supervision of peer ministers and older, trained young adults.	In this stage the new member, who perhaps has been unchurched or apathetic in faith, begins to "catch" the faith of the group. He or she expresses inter-est in more serious study of the Word of God.	P R I M A R Y C O N V E R S I O N (Verbal acceptance of Jesus Christ as Lord and Savior)	Beside weekly small group meetings, the converted or recon-verted young person also attends a weekly study group that studies Scripture and Christian morality.	The desire for an even closer bond with the Lord leads to the search for a spiritual program and prayer life. This stage might be accompanied by Baptism in the Holy Spirit.	Now in the process for two or three years, the older teen recycles to become a leader and guide for younger teens beginning the process or finds other ministry.

activity. Both studies concur in reporting the principal motivating force influencing sexual activity: peer expectations and pressure. One young teenage girl in a video version of the Coles-Stokes study asked, "How can you be eighteen years old and still be a virgin?" The culture, using media amplification, has certainly victimized young people in both understanding and experiencing human sexuality.

To borrow Bettelheim's image, I believe that we as a church need to become a louder voice in the lives of our young people. If we do not, then the other louder voices will continue to mold and shape their inner lives—the voices of consumerism, sexism, and self-actualization. Due to the way that many parish religious education programs are set up, parishes systematically sever ties with their young people as they complete either eighth-grade CCD or parochial school. The sacrament of Confirmation, celebrated in the junior high school years, becomes the equivalent of the ritual of leaving the Church for too many teens. In some of his seminars around the country, Catholic youth expert Don Kimball speaks of a deeper problem: many young people arrive in their teen years in an unevangelized state. Whether they have had formal religious education in their elementary school years or not seems to have little influence. Not only does the parish lose contact with its teenagers, but what the parish does with them during childhood also seems to be questionable in terms of evangelization.

F.L.A.M.E.:
A Catholic Approach to Youth Evangelization

While I have difficulty with the theology and some of the strategies of evangelical youth programs, I do see value in their systematic, wholistic approach to youth. What is probably obvious to the reader in the diagram of full-cycle evangelization presented on page 100 is that many of these evangelical models are catechumenate-like in nature. Youth ministry is a process that begins with social and evangelization efforts, proceeds into deeper religious education, and then goes on to discipleship, commitment, and ministry. The Catholic tradition has all of the pieces of such a systematic approach. We simply need to get them in the right order, and to have patience as we attempt to gradually build quality youth programs.

Dawn Mayer, the associate director of the Office for Chicago Catholic Evangelization, and I have piloted several Catholic versions of full-cycle youth evangelization around the Chicago metropolitan area. We have entitled these pilot programs F.L.A.M.E. The title is an attempt to package youth ministry in nonschooling terminology. Each letter of the title stands for an important ingredient in the whole effort.

Friendship—All youth ministry is relational in nature, both in terms of peer-to-peer and intergenerational ministries.

Leadership—While adults have a role in helping young people organize and develop programs, gradually the programs must be owned by the young people themselves.

A Process—Like the evangelical models and the catechumenate, effective youth ministry is a process of conversion.

Ministry—The process is designed to help both youth and adults discern and use their gifts for the good of young people.

Education—The process of education is, in a broad sense, an attempt to lead young people in the direction of the Kingdom of God.

In the various sites where F.L.A.M.E. is operative, it is being offered as a regional program. In other words, several Catholic parishes in each area are pooling resources and personnel and, in at least some of the offerings, are programming together. Such a regional model is one that more and more parishes ought to consider. A youth effort can be greatly enriched by the young people of several parishes coming together. The general movements of the F.L.A.M.E. process are shown in the diagram on page 103.

The F.L.A.M.E. process can also be viewed from the perspective of the unique needs of young people that each stage of the process addresses, and the way in which the gospel speaks to their needs. These needs and responses are shown in the diagram on page 104.

THE CONFIRMATION CONTROVERSY

If any of our seven sacraments has a fuzzy history and now a diffuse identity, it is the sacrament of Confirmation. Across the country, controversy rages about where to best place the sacrament. Liturgical purists favor either joining it again with Baptism, resulting, perhaps, in the eventual Baptism and Confirmation of infants, or delaying Baptism until adulthood. Religious educators lean toward a delayed age for Confirmation, but many make the mistake of placing it at a certain age or grade level, still maintaining the class or herd mentality that is present in so many junior

STAGES OF THE F.L.A.M.E. PROCESS

Stage 1: Social Ministry and Evangelization	Stage 2: Faith Formation	Stage 3: Personal Group Guidance and Spiritual Direction	Stage 4: The Sacrament of Confirmation	Stage 5: Post-Confirmation Follow-up Activity
• Monthly social events and meetings • Gradual formation of small communities or teams • Training of peer leaders • Evangelization-oriented retreat intended to awaken young people to the difference God can make in life • Small groups generated via the organic growth model	• A nonschooling approach to religious education consisting of: **a.** Monthly seminars that apply the gospel to youth concerns (stress, rock, substance abuse, suicide, friendship) **b.** Follow-up home meetings on deeper religious questions (morality, sexuality, Jesus, death, afterlife)	• For one year prior to Confirmation, a period of deepened discipleship consisting of: **a.** Development of a personal spiritual program **b.** Discernment of personal gifts **c.** Participation in service projects and acts of mercy	• A ritual that retrieves the original meaning of the word *sacrament*, that is, "vow" • A ritual of commitment to Jesus, the Kingdom, and the Body of Christ • An ungraded approach to the ritual (The sacrament is celebrated when ministers and young people feel that stages 1, 2, and 3 have been successfully accomplished.)	• Confirmed young people discern ministries in which they will serve. • Seminars, potlucks, retreats, and overnights provide advanced young people with ongoing faith formation. • Confirmed young people recycle to become leaders for others.

PRIMARY EVANGELIZATION — SECONDARY EVANGELIZATION

YOUTH NEEDS AND GOSPEL RESPONSE

	Stage 1	Stage 2	Stage 3	Stage 4	Stage 5
NEEDS	• Healthy self-concept • Beginning understanding of human sexuality • Belonging to and participation in groups • Positive environment	• Guidance in moral and vocational life choices • Direction in sexuality and intimacy • Guidance in the valuing process • Insights into the meaning of life	• Ideological commitment vs. values confusion	• Psychological, sociological, spiritual need to express, ritualize, symbolize	• Invest creative energies • Discover personal gifts • Transcend self
GOSPEL RESPONSE	• "Be willing to grow and become." • "Come, follow me." • "I challenge you to be different from others." • "I will always be with you." • "I have a new vision of life for you." • "You are loved by the Father." • "Your life is a gift." • "You are loved by the community." • "I can give you a new power for life." • "You belong to this community; I dwell here."	• Systematic exploration of the mysteries of our tradition • God as parent • God's unconditional love • Jesus: Lord and Savior, Brother and Friend • The Spirit; Power, Presence, Strength, Healing • The many models of Church • Morality as responsibility for life • Sacraments • God's unique call to each of us (vocation) • Scripture • Paschal mystery • Prayer	• "Come and be disciples." • "Pray like this." • "Leave all for me." • "Sell what you have and give to the poor." • "Love your enemies." • "Do this in memory of me."	• "Unless you are born again in the water and the Spirit, you cannot see the Reign of God."	• "Go into the world." • "Be salt, light, and leaven." • "Wash feet ... as I have."

high Confirmation programs. The F.L.A.M.E. model stresses an ungraded celebration of Confirmation that happens after passing through stages 1, 2, and 3, and after discernment with a variety of adult ministers in the process.

I do not sense any major shifts being announced from the Vatican regarding Confirmation being joined to Baptism, except in the case of the Rite of Christian Initiation of Adults. Confirmation will probably continue to have its own identity as a separate sacramental ritual. As Church, we have to ask a practical question: Where would this ritual do the most good? In my estimation, it can do the most good as the energizing force within a full-cycle youth evangelization process.

This F.L.A.M.E. approach to Confirmation also integrates into a meaningful whole the various theologies of Confirmation. These theologies, in fact, support and complement each other. The major theological approaches maintain that Confirmation is:
- one's personal completion of initiation into the Church,
- one's owning of responsibility for the mission of the Church,
- a celebration and realization of Jesus' promise that the Holy Spirit will always be with us,
- a celebration of maturing faith, and
- a celebration of the beginning of Christian adulthood.

Delayed-age Confirmation can integrally celebrate all of these theologies of the sacrament.

ADULT MINISTRIES

A full-cycle youth ministry, like F.L.A.M.E., needs a variety of people and gifts to make it all happen. In the F.L.A.M.E. model, Dawn Mayer and I lead adult volunteers through a summer discernment process, explaining various ministerial needs and asking those interested to try to match their abilities with articulated areas of need. Adult ministries may be divided into three categories:
- *Social ministers.* The role of these adults is to help a team or small group of youth to organize social events for itself as well as for the other small communities on occasion.
- *Religious education ministers.* These adults are the ministers of the Word in the small communities. Working with the youth minister(s), they help search out resources and plan seminars, overnights, retreats, and home discussions. (In the F.L.A.M.E. model, at least two adults from each of these first two ministries should be present in each small community.)

- *Spiritual directors.* These adults care for the third stage of the process, the period of discipleship. Spiritual directors, working one on one with teens as well as in groups, focus on prayer, worship, development of a spiritual life, service projects, and ministry. Because the youth in any small group move on to stage 3 at different times, these adult ministers function outside of the small, original faith community. Teens at stage 3 attend meetings with their spiritual director in addition to their ongoing involvement in the original small group.

Social ministers, religious education ministers, and spiritual directors require different styles of training. Social ministers need to learn organizations skills. Religious education ministers need instruction in catechetical methodology. Spiritual directors need training in human relation skills, discernment, prayer, and the use of Scripture.

PEER MINISTERS

The United States Catholic Conference's 1976 Vision Statement on Youth Ministry challenges us to keep in mind that youth ministry must always be "to, for, with, and by youth." In the F.L.A.M.E. model, each small group should have one or two peer leaders who, with the adult ministers, nurture the faith community and add to its members, using the previously described organic growth model of invitation. Summer seminars can be used to train young people in how to listen, how to run meetings, how to advertise events, how to use the telephone for outreach to all parish teens, how to plan prayer and liturgy, and other skills needed to keep the communities alive. Teens who wish to be leaders in ways other than group leaders can minister in committee structures: social events, fund raising, liturgy, retreats, social justice. These standing committees work and plan for the well-being of the entire network of youth communities.

CREATING FEEDER SYSTEMS

A truly wholistic approach to youth ministry necessitates ministering to more than high school adolescents. A high school age program can be strong only if ministry is going on with junior high students. Social events and retreats, as well as religious education, should be offered to both parochial school and public school students. Similarly, graduation from high school should not mean a severing of ties with the young adult. A wholistic model also includes young adult ministries, which are quite complex in that there are so many subpopulations within the generic category of young adults. These may be categorized as follows:

- *18- to 22-year-olds.* These years mark the transition to young adulthood, with some young people going off to college, others living at home and commuting to college, and still others beginning to work. The parish can stay in contact with those in college via the mail and campus visitation, as well as offer programs for those still living in the area.
- *22- to 25-year-olds.* These years mark the beginning of commitments in career and intimacy for many people. Social and educational events should target these major shifts in young people's lives.
- *25- to 33-year-olds.* Many young people speak of these as years of reevaluation. They are years characterized by a high divorce rate and by job change. Again, the parish can address the unique needs of this age group through social and formation programs.
- *33- to 35-year-olds.* These years mark a period of settling down for many, as young adulthood gives way to the beginning of mid-life. Ministry to singles as well as support for marriage and family life is important during these years.

This brief analysis indicates that young adult ministry will fail if we do not take into account the pluralism and diversity of the young adult population. Young adults also need to be ministered to "on their turf." Some parishes have begun condominium and apartment ministries in an attempt to gather young adults for social, educational, or prayer experiences.

MINISTRY TO TROUBLED YOUTH

The International Youth for Christ movement has a second tract besides its mainline ministry for young people seeking the Lord. Too often we attract relatively healthy kids to our youth programs with little attention to the young people most in need of Christ: the addicted, the runaway, the neurotic, or the depressed young person. Counseling and spiritual direction services are offered at regional centers in the Youth for Christ movement. The goal of these centers is to engage in a ministry of healing and reconciliation with hurting young people. Again, as Catholics we have much to learn from Protestant and evangelical models, if we are to develop wholistic youth evangelization.

5

The Catechumenal Parish

The second chapter of the Acts of the Apostles reveals one style of evangelization and invitation in the early Church. After Peter delivered a proclamation of the gospel, his listeners were led to conversion to the risen Lord Jesus. This conversion was expressed or ritualized in the water bath of Baptism. Christian growth took place after Baptism, through teaching, fellowship, Eucharist, and prayer. This New Testament pattern consisted of evangelization, sacramental moment, and a process of Christian growth. By the middle of the second century, another pattern became very popular in certain centers of Christianity. This pattern consisted of community outreach, proclamation of the Good News followed by a kind of primary or first conversion, a request for entrance into the community, a period of discernment or examination of the candidate's life, profession of faith, a period of immediate preparation for initiation or Baptism, and ongoing growth through teaching, worship, and acts of charity. We now call this process the catechumenate, or Rite of Christian Initiation of Adults.

Moving into the third century, two rather major portions of this process of initiation became evident: a period of discipleship and a period of election or being chosen by the community. Discipleship was entered into by a brief ceremony that included the imposition of hands and blessing with the sign of the cross. The period of election was a period of proximate preparation for initiation. In many areas, this entire preparation took up to three years. A key ingredient in the process was discernment (prayerful watching, waiting, observing, and praying). The object of discernment was always the depth and quality of conversion in a candidate's life. The catechumenate reached its golden age in the third century. Notice the difference between the catechumenal model of evangelization, conversion, and initiation and the New Testament model of Acts. The Acts 2 model places the process of growth after the sacrament. The later catechumenal model places the process of conversion before the celebration of initiation, with continued growth after initiation. The Rite of Christian Initiation of Adults, prescribed by the Second Vatican Council and released in January 1972, recaptures the richness of the third-century catechumenate. The RCIA was translated into English and released in America in 1974.

By the fourth century, the catechumenate began to erode qualitatively and quantitatively. Though remnants of it remained in the centers of Christianity into the seventh and eighth centuries and beyond, the rich process of conversion of the third century was greatly diminished. Several converging factors contributed to its demise.

1. Emperor Constantine's ceasing of the persecution of Christians and, later, Emperor Theodosius's naming Christianity as the state religion did much to foster what we might call today "cultural Christianity." A person was at a disadvantage socially, economically, and interpersonally if he or she were not a Christian. Mass Baptisms and Baptisms of households became commonplace. In effect, people were baptized with little regard as to whether conversion had been experienced.

2. The dynamic of discernment, so crucial to the process in its golden age, gave way to a depersonalized approach to catechesis.

3. The clericalization of ministries, centering them all in the bishop or the priest, robbed the catechumenate of it synergism, its collective energy that came from a variety of different ministers working together to complement each other. In an attempt to clarify doctrine in the face of many heresies, the bishop or his representative more and more took on the role of the teacher or catechist.

4. The two threshold moments of primary conversion, when one became a catechumen, and secondary conversion, when one began the period of proximate preparation, became insignificant. In some areas by the fourth and fifth centuries, the catechumenate was relegated to the weeks before Easter, or what we now know as Lent.

5. The delicate balance between education, ministry, guidance and sponsorship, and rituals that congruently expressed actual conversion was lost. Specifically the marriage between Word and ritual was broken. The importance of catechumens' serving as sacramental reminders of conversion to the rest of the community was lost sight of as the ritual, liturgical steps of initiation were abandoned.

6. The Baptism of infants became popularized as the theory of original sin was developed, and the necessity of Baptism for eternal life provided assurance to mothers living in an age of high infant mortality.

I present this brief historical analysis with concern for the Church of today. What the catechumenate offered to the Church in the second and third centuries and what it offers to us today is at the heart of what an evangelizing parish tries to be and do. With the erosion of the catechumenate, the Church lost its countercultural, conversion-oriented, communal characteristics. They were replaced by institutionalization, dogma, clericalism, and a superficial, cultural kind of Christianity. This continues to be the state of the Church in too many parishes in our country and around the world. Parishes need to get beyond the RCIA as some kind of easy, facile program, to the values and principles that permeated Christian communities centuries ago. It is those catechumenal values and principles that can transform the typical parish into an evangelizing parish.

LEARNING FROM THE CATECHUMENATE

In Chapter 2, in the section headed "Constant Six: Renewal of Calendars," I discussed the possibility of translating the stages or steps of the catechumenate into similar steps in other ministries: sacramental preparation, youth ministry, adult and family education, and so on. Let us consider those steps or stages: (1) evangelization and awakening of faith (followed by discernment and conversion), (2) catechesis or faith enriched with deeper understanding (followed by discernment and conversion), (3) deepened discipling and proximate preparation for commitment, (4) sacrament, conversion, commitment, (5) ongoing deepening of faith.

These steps are natural steps in religious socialization and growth. Anthropological studies reveal similar steps in the education strategies of non-Christian religions. From a pragmatic point of view, the steps are an effective way to bring about life change, and can be adapted for many purposes in the parish. But beyond pragmatic strategies, the RCIA has much more to teach contemporary parishes. Among these important lessons are the following:

1. Conversion takes time.   Typical parish programs, like adult education, offer compartmentalized units of information or formation, but few provide the luxury of time that the catechumenate does. The catechumenate is a process that a small community engages in and experiences together. The biblical image of "journey" is the metaphor that best summarizes catechumenal time.

2. The parish should focus on adults.   While many programs can be offered for children and families, the faith life of the parish will be only as strong as the faith of the adult community. Adults need to be aided in making sense of life through the gospel.

3. Sacraments are about conversion.   We have robbed sacraments of their power by seeing them as things rather than as ritual expressions of ongoing conversion. Contemporary disciples need to be helped beyond "cheap grace" sacraments to see sacraments as catechumens do: opportunities to vow to the Lord and the Body of Christ.

4. Small is beautiful.   We have discussed in other sections of this book how the anonymity of many parishes makes true community and faith sharing impossible. The small group experience of the RCIA, in which faith is "caught" in shared lives, stories, and relationships, ought to be reduplicated in as many parish efforts as possible.

5. Ministries and ministers can function cooperatively.   Conversion happens in the catechumenate because of the harnessed gifts and energies of many people. In an RCIA process that is working effectively, ministries of the Word, worship, and accompaniment (or guidance) function together toward the common goal of conversion.

6. The community is the sacrament of God's presence.   In the catechumenate, conversion is synonymous with entrance into the community. The community is seen as the tabernacle of God's presence and center of God's wisdom, healing, and truth. So, conversion to Jesus and the Kingdom is always via the Body of Christ.

7. Spirituality is paschal in nature.   The catechumenate reminds the rest of the parish of the true nature of baptismal spirituality.

We have been baptized into the death of Christ, so that we might also share in His resurrection. True conversion is life, death, and resurrection in, with, and through Jesus over and over again.

8. Conversion is the work of the Holy Spirit. While the community and various ministers of the RCIA process create an environment in which conversion can take place, the true agent of conversion is the Holy Spirit. Conversion is a movement of the Holy Spirit. Paul Tillich, a theologian, used to speak of conversion as being grasped by the Spirit. The catechumenate renews awareness of and dependence on the Holy Spirit.

9. There is a mutuality in true ministry. Catechumens are a good example of all people who are recipients of the parish's ministry. In their being cared for by the community, they begin to minister back to others and the community. In effect, their search and struggle for conversion remind each person in the parish of the ongoing call to conversion.

10. Discernment is a vital part of conversion. Instant gratification and results are so much a part of our culture that we sometimes bring that instantaneous mind-set to faith. We sometimes think that religious programs should bring about the desired results as quickly as hot water can transform coffee granules. True spiritual growth involves a great deal of groping, searching, becoming lost, and then finding the way again. Discernment, that is, slow and prayerful watching in community, is vital to both discovering who will do what ministry in a parish and monitoring the faith growth of each other.

CONCLUSION

More than "starting a catechumenate," the community that is becoming an evangelizing parish is catechumenal in nature. The catechumenal parish both adapts the RCIA steps of religious socialization for many parish efforts and applies these and other catechumenal principles to parish ministries.

INDEX

Adler, Alfred, 83
Alienation, reasons for, 64–72
Anonymity, problem of in Catholic
    Church, 36, 41–42, 43

Barth, Karl, 36
Base communities, 45–46
Bell, Joe, 97
Bettelheim, Bruno, 99
Bishops' synod in Rome (1974), 6–8
Black Catholics, 39
Braxton, Edward, 45–46

Carkhuff, Robert, 78
Catechumenal parish, 109–13
    flow chart of, 58–59
Catechumenate. See Rite of Christian
    Initiation of Adults
Catholicism Revisited, 89, 91–93
Clark, Stephen, 45–46
Coles, Robert, 99–100
Confirmation, 102, 105
Conscientization, 36–37
Constantine, 110
Convergence evangelization, 15–16, 49
Conversion, 20–21, 109–13

Discernment, 53, 109–10, 113
    of needs, 27–30, 87, 89
Discipleship, 21–22, 109
Dreikurs, Rudolf, 38
Dunning, Jim, 49
Durkin, Mary Greeley, 41, 69

Egan, Gerard, 78
Erikson, Erik, 98
Evangelicalism, 1–4
    evangelizing strategies of, 2–4
    growth of evangelical churches, 18

strengths of, 4
    youth movements in, 39–40
Evangelii Nuntiandi, 8–12, 20, 23, 36,
    39, 63
Evangelization
    of active parishioners, 23–61
    of adults, 30–31, 112
    attitude of, 17
    beneficiaries of, 10
    of blacks, 39
    and the Church, 17
    concerns about, 7–8
    content of, 9
    convergence, 15–16, 49
    in early Church, 109–11
    foundational, 14–15, 45
    of Hispanics, 26, 38–39
    and the Holy Spirit, 11, 16–17
    of inactive or alienated parishioners,
        63–96
    Jesus' style of, 8, 17, 21–22, 37
    meaning of word, 5, 6–7, 14
    methods of doing, 9
    mission of, 8–9, 16
    obstacles to, 6
    prompted by love, 11
    strategies of, 18
    witness in, 11
    of youth, 11, 14, 39–41, 97–107
Evangelization of the Modern World,
    The, 6–8
"Event evangelization," 26–27

Falwell, Jerry, 2
Familiaris Consortio, 32
F.L.A.M.E., 101–3, 105, 106
Foley, Leonard, 2
Forliti, John, 89
Foundational evangelization, 14–15, 45

Fowler, James, 98
Freire, Paulo, 37
Freud, Sigmund, 83
Fundamentalism, 1–4

Gallup, George, Jr., 66
Gordon, Thomas, 78
Greeley, Andrew, 41, 68–69
Groome, Thomas, 37
Guzie, Tad, 32

Hale, J. Russell, 67–68
Hass, Aaron, 99–100
Hispanic Catholics, 26, 38–39
Hoge, Dean, 69–71
Holmes, Urban, 85
Homecoming, 89–91
Hubbard, Howard, 32
Humanae Vitae, 68–69

Illig, Alvin, 17

Jesus
    and style of evangelization, 8, 17,
        21–22, 37
    and style of ministry, 63
John Paul II, 32

Kimball, Don, 14, 101
Kingdom of God, 17, 19–20
Kleissler, Thomas, 46
Kohlberg, Lawrence, 98

Leadership, 48, 50–55
    parish council, 52–53
Leadership magazine, 85
Leege, David, 60–61
Liégé, Pierre-Andre, 12–13
Liturgy, improving, 35–36

McBrien, Richard, 23
McCready, William, 38
Maslow, Abraham, 36
Maximum influence, principle of,
    18–19, 41
Mayer, Dawn, x, 101–2, 105
Ministry
    board of, 50–52
    calling, 73–76
    of care and reconciliation, 72–73
    to inactive or alienated members,
        64–96

Jesus' style of, 63
    neighborhood, 42–45
    pastoral care, 37–38
    recruitment for, 53–54
    renewal of, 46–48
    training for, 54
Mission
    developing a sense of, 56–57
    of evangelization, 8–9, 16
    parish, 26–27
Multiplication, principle of, 18–19, 41
Murnion, Philip, 36

Naisbitt, John, 48
National Council for Catholic
        Evangelization, 15
Navarro, Alphonsus, 45
Nebreda, Alfonso, 12–13
Need discernment, 27–30, 87, 89
Neighborhood ministry, 42–45
Neurolinguistics, 35, 77–78

O'Meara, Thomas, 46

Palmer, Parker, 37
Pastoral care ministries, 37–38
Paul VI, 8–12, 16, 19, 20, 23, 63, 68–69
Pentecost, 16–17
Peter, 16–17
Peters, Tom, 18, 48
Politicization, 37
Prayer, 57, 60–61
Preevangelization, 13
Priesthood, 47–48

Rauff, Edward, 35, 36
Religious education
    adult, 30–31
    family-based, 31–32, 33–34
    sacramental programs, 32–34
Renew, 23
Renewal, 23–61
    of calendars, 55–56
    of ministry, 46–48
    of parish structures, 48–55
    of parish vision, 24–27
    of prayer life, 57, 60–61
    and renewed priorities, 27–41
    through small faith-sharing
        groups, 41–46
    of tone, 56–57
"Revival, the," 26–27

Rite of Christian Initiation of
   Adults (RCIA), 32, 49, 55–56,
   91–92, 105, 109–13

Sacramental preparation, 32–34
Savage, John, 71–72
Searle, Mark, 60–61
Second Vatican Council, 8
   documents of, 13
Skills, relational, 76–96
   developing reconciling responses,
      80–83
   faith sharing, 85–86
   follow-up, 95
   handling objections, questions,
      anger, 93–94
   information gathering, 86–87
   invitation, 89
   listening, 78–79, 84–85
   need discernment, 87, 89
   networking, 87
   supporting fellow callers, 94–95
   time lining a visit, 94
   using body language, 76–78
   using paraphrase and reflection
      back, 79–80
Social justice consciousness, 36–37
Stokes, Geoffrey, 99–100
Structuring, 48–55

Suenens, Cardinal, vii
Sweetser, Tom, 42

Torrey, R. A., 1
Training, for ministry of reconciliation,
   64–96
   contracting for visit, 73–76
   skills for relating, 76–96
   understanding why people leave,
      64–73

Vision (mission) statement
   developing, 24–26
   of parish groups, 20

Welsh, John R., 46
Women, role of, 38

Youth, evangelization of, 11, 14, 39–41,
   97–107
   adult ministries for, 105–6
   F.L.A.M.E., 101–3, 105, 106
   full-cycle, 98–100
   organic growth model of, 39–40, 98
   peer ministries in, 106
   strategies for, 98–101
   troubled youth, 107
   young adult ministries for, 106–7